Survey of the New Testament

Nondisposable Curriculum

J. Kie Bowman

Auxano Press

Auxano
PRESS

Tigerville, South Carolina

i

Dedication

Dedicated to the believer who seeks the Lord, loves His Word, and always expects the epic adventure of whatever God does next.

ISBN 978-0-578-05752-9

Published by Auxano Press
Tigerville, South Carolina
www.AuxanoPress.com

CONTENTS

ACKNOWLEDGMENTS

I want to thank Dr. Ken Hemphill for inviting me to write this companion volume to his *Old Testament Survey*. He has been a friend who has blessed me for many years on numerous occasions. Partnering with Auxano Press on this project is one of the clearest and most recent examples. He has honored me with the opportunity to write this work.

In addition, I want to express my deepest gratitude to Hyde Park Baptist Church and The Quarries Church (one church in two locations) in Austin, Texas, where I have served as senior pastor since 1997. They give me abundant freedom, which has allowed me the time to work on this volume; and I know they were praying for me as I studied and wrote. I love my church!

Three individuals who helped me along the way deserve much more than this simple word of thanks: Becky Shipp serves as my executive assistant and typed, proofed, and waited on this manuscript; and I am greatly appreciative of her work on a daily basis. Marita Murphy reviewed most of the manuscript and offered important and helpful improvements in a timely manner. Toni Casteel also worked on a portion of it with equal insight and alacrity. These three women were a joy to work with, and I am grateful to each of them.

Finally, my wife, Tina, patiently endured my constant conversation about deadlines (most of which I missed) and listened as I discussed what I was learning, much of which was far too detailed to be included in the final draft. I honestly think she was happier when I finished than I was. Thank you, Tina, for exercising your gift of long-suffering through this sometimes all-consuming project. I promise I will not start a new project for at least a few days!

As in Dr. Hemphill's Old Testament volume, I have limited the use of direct quotations. Still, I am indebted to far superior works that have preceded this one. Four of those deserve special mention: The New American Commentary, The Bible Speaks Today commentary series (especially John R. W. Stott's volume on the Acts of the Apostles), The Tyndale New Testament Commentaries, and the *Holman Illustrated Bible Dictionary*. Each was close by throughout this project and influenced many of my conclusions.

Finally, I am extremely grateful to God for calling me to a life that allows me so much time to study the Bible. I hope my appreciation is obvious in the work I have done here.

INTRODUCTION

When I was chosen to write this *Survey*, my assignment was simple: choose twelve passages or events that tell the story of the New Testament. Of course, that assignment is anything but simple. Any fifty writers could have chosen a hundred different configurations of the material other than the way I finally arranged it here. In my early planning I had multiple lists of possible chapters, and the question was always, What do I leave out? There is an abundance of material to choose from, and the New Testament is the most well-known, well-researched, beloved, and—along with the Old Testament—best-selling book in history. The task of what to include, therefore, was never easy and might have been done another way.

The final chapter selections, however, were chosen to tell the story of Jesus and the movement He started. As John reminds us, "Jesus did many other things as well. If every one of them were written down, I suppose that even the whole world would not have room for the books that would be written" (John 21:25, NIV). In a way John's hyperbole has proven true since more has been written about Jesus of Nazareth than any other person who has ever lived. This current project is my small contribution to the world full of literature amassed about the greatest life ever lived. My prayer is that this will be a blessing to those who want a better understanding of the greatest story ever told.

My reasons for choosing the passages that form the structure of this work were based on certain presuppositions and principles. First, the New Testament has a central character—Jesus of Nazareth. Most of these chapters, therefore, focus on events in the Gospels. I made no effort to equally divide the stories from the four Gospels. Instead, I relied on the most detailed or familiar versions of the stories among the four Gospels, which were frequently found in Matthew. Jesus is the main character of this work. Writing these chapters was a personal, devotional exercise and a true labor of love.

The second principle guiding the selection of material is that the New Testament is the story of a movement—the rapid growth of the early church in the first century AD in the Roman Empire. Much more can be said about the material in Acts through Revelation and will be covered by future Auxano books in the Nondisposable Curriculum series, but the stories chosen here are meant to give the reader a general, but focused, overview.

Finally, I did not write this volume for other preachers or for my former seminary professors. I am a pastor. I preach more than a hundred sermons a year, and I work every Sunday to communicate not to scholars of the Bible but to fellow students like me. I thought of that audience as I wrote—people who want to know more about the Bible and who share a passion to learn. I wrote this volume from a pastor's study and from a pastor's heart. As a pastor, I have known hundreds of people over the years who, lacking formal training, have nevertheless gained a mind full of truth because they have hearts hungry for the message of Scripture. This New Testament Survey is written for them. It is written for you.

J. Kie Bowman
Austin, Texas
January 2013

The Birth of Jesus

Focal Text: Matthew 1–2

Almost everybody loves Christmas. The malls decorate for it, the radio stations play its music, we gather as families to celebrate it, and we have lasting memories throughout our lives from Christmas. We know why we love Christmas with its traditions, food, and celebration; but what is the scriptural purpose of telling the story of the birth of Jesus?

The Fulfillment of Prophesy

Of the four Gospels only two detail the Christmas story. Both Matthew and Luke emphasize how the birth of Jesus was the fulfillment of Old Testament messianic prophecy. Luke makes this clear in subtle ways through the speeches of Zechariah, Mary, Simeon, Anna, and the angels, which are all loaded with Old Testament references and allusions. Matthew, however, is much less subtle. In fact, Matthew contains an abundance of Old Testament references, half of which do not occur in any of the other Gospels.[1] He tells the story of the birth of Jesus stating five times that the events are the result of "what has been written by the prophet" (Matt. 2:5).

God with Us (1:18–25)

The first prophetic fulfillment involves the well-known dilemma of Joseph's discovering that Mary was having a child. Matthew weaves a brief but compelling narrative from a human drama told against the backdrop of a love story, a misun-

1

derstanding, and the possibility of a betrayal. While Joseph is considering the merits of a private divorce, an angel intervenes and insists that God is at work in spite of the apparent circumstances.

The angel then instructs Joseph to assume the role of husband to Mary and father to her unborn baby, giving Him the name "Jesus" because "He will save His people from their sins" (v 21). The name *Jesus* means "Jehovah is salvation."

Matthew's story of Joseph and the angel not only looks forward to the naming of the child to be born; it also looks back to a prophecy written hundreds of years earlier. In verse 23, Matthew quotes Isaiah 7:14, which promises a virgin birth as a sign from God.

The virgin birth is also taught explicitly in Luke's version of the birth narrative. In both passages it is associated with giving the baby the name "Jesus" (Luke 1:31–34). Isaiah did not say the child would be named "Jesus," nor does Matthew suggest that he did, but Matthew reminds his readers that Isaiah said, "They shall call His name Immanuel." And then adds, "which translated means 'God with us'" (v. 23). "Immanuel," therefore is seen more as a description of the child's character or function, rather than as an actual name in the normal sense.

In the first of Matthew's many references to Old Testament prophesies, therefore, he finds a promise of God's presence with His people. While nowhere in Scripture is God absent from history, in the birth of Jesus, we find the presence of God revealed in a way that most conforms to our own sense of reality. He became one of us. God is near.

When Matthew wrote his Gospel, the faith of the early church was being challenged by the religious and civil authorities. Just as it is today in many parts of the world and to a lesser degree in the United States, standing for Christ was not easy.

The first point in Matthew's "Christmas sermon," therefore, is the assurance that no matter how alienated, persecuted, or rejected we may feel, we will always be welcome in God's presence. As John Wesley declared on his deathbed, "The best of all is, God is with us."

The Shepherd King (2:1–12)

The second prophetic fulfillment occurs in the midst of one of the most familiar and beloved of the Christmas' stories. The magi were a group of Eastern wise men or priests from ancient Persia or Babylon, roughly equivalent to modern-day Iran and Iraq. From their study of the night sky and possibly the ancient prophecies of Jewish literature, they became convinced that the appearance of a new star, which moved from east to west, was the herald of the new King of the Jews.

How did the magi know the significance of the star? Had they themselves discovered the prediction of a rising star as they studied Old Testament prophecy? Numbers 24:17 says, "I see him, but not now; I behold him, but not near; a star shall come forth from Jacob, a scepter shall rise from Israel."

We cannot know with certainty how the magi knew the King of Israel was being born or how they knew the star would guide them to Him. We are confident, however, that God was revealing it to them. By contrast the leaders of Israel did not know the King had been born. King Herod wasted no time getting answers. A paranoid leader, he assembled his religious advisors. He needed to know where the "King of the Jews" would be born. The answer was easy for the teachers: "In Bethlehem of Judea; for this is what has been written by the prophet: 'And you, Bethlehem, land of Judah, are by no means least among the leaders of Judah; for out of you shall come forth a Ruler

3

who will shepherd My people Israel'" (vv. 5–6).

Bethlehem was a tiny town in the first century. It was not on the main road. It was known mainly for agriculture, sheep, and as the hometown of Israel's greatest king, David. A few other biblical stories are related to Bethlehem, but the prominence of Bethlehem rested in the prediction involving a future ruler, a "shepherd" for Israel.

The birth of the "shepherd King" is a lesson in contrasts. Five miles away in Jerusalem, Herod was clinging to power, living in luxury. He was entertaining Eastern dignitaries from the courts of Persia or Babylon. Yet he was oblivious to the impoverished couple who had delivered their first child and laid Him in a "manger" (Luke 2:7). With God small things can be made great, but what looks great at the moment may suddenly collapse.

The King God sent for His people would not be a tyrant like Herod. Instead He would be a shepherd, a caring pastor, and someone with humble origins who relates to the common problems of every person.

Out of Egypt (2:13–15)

The third fulfillment from the Old Testament is from an obscure verse found in the prophet Hosea: "When Israel was a youth I loved him, and out of Egypt I called My son" (Hos. 11:1).

While Jesus and His family were still in Bethlehem, an angel communicated with Joseph for a second time. This time, rather than being assured by the angel, Joseph received an urgent warning regarding Herod's plan to kill the child. He was told to go south to Egypt.

How does Hosea's comment concerning the historical exodus of the nation of Israel relate to the flight of Jesus into and out of Egypt? Hosea 11:1 is not a prediction. Instead, it refers to

4

God's historic preservation of Israel. It also refers to the nation as God's "Son."

In the Old Testament the entire nation was called God's "Son" (Exod. 4:22–23). The first time that occurs is in relationship to God's call to leave Egypt. As time passed, the prophets began to see that the "Son," represented by the nation of Israel, would ultimately be embodied by one man (2 Sam. 7:14) and that Son would be the King of Israel who will rule over all the earth (Ps. 2:6–9)

Matthew had already begun to develop the emphasis of Jesus as a "Son" (1:21, 23), and twelve times in his gospel he refers to Jesus as "the Son of God."

Matthew's use of Hosea's allusion to Egypt and the Son of God is therefore a reminder that the baby King Herod was attempting to assassinate is the true King of Israel and the true Son of God.

The Suffering of the Innocent (2:16–18)

As the "Christmas sermon" of Matthew continues, he uses a fourth prophecy fulfillment to reveal the true nature and identity of the baby Jesus. This fourth passage is brutal and reminds us of the savage times into which Jesus was born. "Then what had been spoken through Jeremiah the prophet was fulfilled: 'A voice is heard in Ramah, weeping and great mourning, Rachel weeping for her children; and she refused to be comforted, because they are no more" (Matt. 2:17–18).

King Herod was a contradiction in history. He was a brilliant architect who built structures ranging from palaces in the desert to the remodeling project of the temple in Jerusalem. Herod, however, for all of his genius, was a killer. He murdered several family members in order to protect his hold on power. So it should come as no surprise that his brutality could lead to an unthinkable act—he killed every baby boy under the age of two in Bethlehem and the surrounding area (v. 16). In the midst of the carnage, Matthew was reminded of an Old Testament passage from Jeremiah 31:15 describing the inconsolable mourning of a mother who has lost her child.

Jeremiah used the analogy of Rachel weeping for her children as a parable to describe the horror Israel and Judah were enduring while their enemies dominated, destroyed, and enslaved them. Rachel had been the dearly loved wife of Jacob and died while giving birth to Benjamin (Gen. 35:16–19). Her burial place was identified as "on the way to Ephrath (that is, Bethlehem)" and was forever associated with the town. She was loved by the succeeding generations as the suffering mother figure of her "children" Israel.

Jeremiah heard God say that although "Rachel was weeping" her comfort was coming. God would restore the fortunes of Judah and bring the exiles home. Best of all, God promised that He would make a new "covenant" with the people that would transform their hearts and minds, and they would enjoy a deep, intimate relationship with God and the forgiveness of sin (Jer. 31:31–34).

The exact phrase "new covenant" (found nowhere else in the Old Testament) depicts a radical concept because it does not promise a renewal of existing agreements between God and Israel but instead a completely new arrangement that replaces the old covenant God provided at Sinai. Matthew's use of Jeremiah's analogy teaches that Rachel is still weeping for Israel because her children are still brutalized by outside forces but also because her children have not yet been included into the promised "new covenant." Thirty years or so later that Baby, who escaped the execution at the hands of Herod, would say to His disciples, "This is My blood of the new covenant, which is poured out for many for the forgiveness of sins" (Matt. 26:28).

A Nazarene

The fifth and final prophetic fulfillment of the birth narrative refers to Nazareth. Nazareth was a tiny village in the hills of northern Galilee so obscure it was not mentioned in the Old Testament. Even one of Jesus' disciples asked incredulously, "Can any good thing come out of Nazareth?" (John 1:46). It was, however, the perfect place for Jesus to grow up until He could be "manifested [or revealed] to Israel" (John 1:31). "And [He] came and lived in a city called Nazareth. This was to fulfill what was spoken through the prophets: 'He shall be called a Nazarene'" (Matt. 2:23).

Interestingly the Old Testament records no specific prophecy with these words. Even Matthew's familiar formula, "What was said through the prophet," is changed slightly to "through the prophets" with no specific prophet mentioned. So what is Matthew teaching about Jesus and Old Testament prophecy?

The obscurity of Nazareth may be exactly the connection Matthew is making. For instance, regarding the Messiah, Isaiah said: "He grew up before Him like a tender shoot, and like a root out of parched ground; He has no stately form or majesty that we should look upon Him, nor appearance that we should be attracted to Him" (Isa. 53:2).

Psalm 22:6, also a messianic prophecy, portrays the Messiah as "despised by the people." In other words, just as Nazareth was obscure, the Messiah Himself would initially be obscure.

Through these five prophetic fulfillments, Matthew shows us that Jesus is the promised Messiah of Israel, predicted by the prophets, and anticipated by God's people. The birth of Jesus is more than a sentimental holiday, as it sometimes seems to us. He is the fulfillment of all God has promised. Jesus is the One to whom the prophets looked forward. No wonder Jesus alone is "the reason for the season."

For Memory and Meditation

"She will bear a Son, and you shall call His name Jesus, for He will save His people from their sins." Matthew 1:21

---

[1] Craig L. Blomberg, *Matthew*, vol. 22, The New American Commentary (Nashville: Broadman Press, 1992), 30.

John the Baptist

Focal Text: Matthew 3:1–17

In the New Testament perhaps no frequently mentioned character is more mysterious to the contemporary reader than John the Baptist. He seems to have achieved his stated objective, "I must decrease" (John 3:30); yet all four Gospels waste no time introducing him to us. Matthew describes him immediately after the birth narrative of Jesus (Matt. 3:1–17). Mark opens his Gospel with an account of the ministry of John the Baptist (Mark 1:2–8). Luke introduces his Gospel with a long and intricate description of John the Baptist's birth narrative and then picks up the story of John the Baptist as an adult immediately after the birth narrative of Jesus (Luke 1:5–3:20). When the apostle John writes the fourth Gospel, John the Baptist is introduced by name before the name of Jesus is mentioned. The Baptist's story in the fourth Gospel also plays a central role in explaining the early ministry of Jesus (John 1:6–36). The life and ministry of John the Baptist was so exceptional that the religious leaders of his day wondered aloud if he were the coming Christ (John 1:19–20)! Jesus Himself would later say, "Among those born of women there has not arisen anyone greater than John the Baptist!" (Matt. 11:11).

Why did the Gospel writers devote so much attention to John the Baptist? What role did he fulfill that made his brief but unusually effective ministry so impossible to ignore for those who first told the story of Jesus?

The Voice in the Desert
Matthew 3:3

The religious leaders in Jesus' day, the Sadducees and the Pharisees, had made the practice of Judaism nearly impossible for the average person. They were strict, judgmental, and exclusive. They were small sectarian groups representing only about 5 percent of the total population, yet they exercised nearly unquestioned control over religious life and expression. They were ill prepared, however, for the seemingly wild and uncontrolled presence of John the Baptist. Matthew, like the other three Gospels, identified the enigmatic John the Baptist with a quote from the prophet Isaiah: "This is the one referred to by Isaiah the prophet when he said, 'The voice of one crying in the wilderness, make ready the way for the LORD, make His paths straight'" (Matt. 3:3).

Not only did the Gospel writers use this verse to describe him, but John saw himself the same way. In the fourth Gospel, when the baffled religious leaders who did not know what to make of the Baptist asked him who he was, he replied, "I am a voice of one crying in the wilderness" (John 1:23).

The Judean desert is a barren, infertile, and inhospitable place where mercilessly little rainfall, an abundance of rock, and sweltering summer heat leave the landscape so useless for agriculture or livestock that few people ventured to live there. John the Baptist, however, was raised there (Luke 1:80) and spent most of his short but impressive ministry in the desert where the Jordan River meanders down to the Dead Sea. In that quiet theater, where the sound of the wind blowing hot against the sand was nearly the only thing heard, a preacher's cry would have split through the silence like a train whistle cutting through the night air. His message touched a nerve with the spiritually hungry people alienated from the lifeless

10

regulation of the religious class in Jerusalem. They gathered to him from everywhere in the surrounding region (v. 5). He was more than a novelty. He promised that Someone greater was coming from God (v. 3).

The Relationship to Elijah
Matthew 3:4

The Bible rarely gives physical descriptions of the people we know so well. When it does, therefore, we have to decide how it helps the author tell his story.

Both Matthew and Mark (Mark 1:6) give us a partial physical description of John the Baptist, yet neither explains why. Evidently they expected the reader to understand the significance. What, then, is the significance of the seemingly trivial reference to the Baptist's camel-hair clothes and leather belt (Matt. 3:4)?

John the Baptist was obviously a prophetic figure. Jesus Himself described him as, "A prophet? Yes, I tell you, and one who is more than a prophet" (Matt. 11:9). So how do his clothes help us understand him or his mission? The answer is found in the Old Testament in one of the other rare physical descriptions of a biblical character. In an interesting event in 2 Kings, the king of Samaria was inquiring about the appearance of a prophet being discussed by the king's servant. The servant said, "He was a hairy man with a leather girdle bound about his loins." When the king heard that unusual description, he blurted out, "It is Elijah the Tishbite" (2 Kings 1:1–8).

Due to the rarity of physical descriptions in Scripture, it is significant that John the Baptist is also described as wearing "camel's hair and a leather belt around his waist" (Matt. 3:4). We can be certain it is a direct reference to Elijah. It is a sign that

11

the Baptizer was the fulfillment of the prophecy of Malachi 4:5–6, which promised that God would send Elijah the prophet before the "day of the LORD." With that the Old Testament abruptly ends anticipating the appearance of the prophet Elijah. Jesus left no doubt about this in Matthew 11:10 when He said concerning John the Baptist, "This is the one about whom it is written, 'Behold, I send My messenger ahead of You, who will prepare Your way before You.'" Later He was even more direct, "And if you are willing to accept it, John himself is Elijah who was to come" (Matt. 11:14).

John the Baptist therefore plays an essential role in prophetic fulfillment. He came, as the angel told Zechariah his father, "in the spirit and power of Elijah" (Luke 1:17). In order to meet all the criteria of the Jewish Messiah, Jesus had to be preceded by a forerunner (Mal. 4:5). John the Baptist was the man.

The Baptism of Repentance
Matthew 3:6–11

If Matthew were a playwright, the introduction of John the Baptist would provide a memorable scene. Imagine an empty stage and suddenly a wild-looking prophet with a booming voice strides out with no warning shouting one word: "Repent!" From a literary standpoint that's exactly how Matthew introduces John the Baptist. In Luke's Gospel by contrast, we are introduced to John's parents, told about his birth, and given a clue about his calling and anointing (Luke 1:57–80). Matthew gives us no such warnings. Instead, John abruptly enters the stage of history preaching a sermon of repentance (Matt. 3:1). Following forty days of fasting in the Judean desert, after learning that John had been arrested, Jesus began His preaching ministry with the identical message John had preached,

"Repent, for the kingdom of heaven is near" (Matt. 4:17).

In addition to preaching, John's unusual ministry included baptism in the Jordan River (Matt. 3:6–11). The ritual of baptism by immersion was not unknown or even uncommon to first-century Jews. Large impressive "baptisteries" called "mikvahs," used for full-body immersion, can still be seen in Jerusalem around the Temple Mount and at Qumran where the eclectic puritan group known as the Essenes lived and studied Scripture. As a ritual of cleansing before entering the temple for worship, Jews would immerse themselves. The Essenes of Qumran immersed themselves twice a day, morning and evening, as a symbol of moral cleansing. John the Baptist, by comparison, may have been the first person in history to immerse others. His baptism was in the Jewish tradition of demonstrating outwardly the inward commitment of the heart toward God and His law (v. 6). John's baptism, however, was not merely an oft-repeated ritual but instead an urgent action in response to the warning to "flee from the wrath to come" (v. 7).

The Holy Spirit and Fire

Everything about John the Baptist projected a rugged individualism: he seemed fearless, and his temperament appeared harsh. He saw the world as bad and getting worse, and only one thing could change it—repentance (Matt. 3:7–10; Luke 3:7–9). John was not a warm, pastoral teacher; he was a thunderclap of prophetic energy.

John the Baptist's rough exterior melted one day when Jesus of Nazareth presented Himself as a candidate for John's baptism (Matt. 3:14). John had appeared with an authority not seen in Israel since the days of the prophets hundreds of years earlier, but he was keenly aware of his inferiority to the One who was to come next. John saw himself as less than a slave and lacking the status necessary even to exercise the menial, and in some ways demeaning, task of carrying a master's dirty sandals (Matt. 3:11).

Not only was he aware of his personal inferiority to Jesus; he recognized the vast superiority of Jesus' ministry as well. John was self-effacing when he pointed out that his baptism was only "with water" while the baptism of Jesus would be "with the Holy Spirit and fire" (v. 11). The term "baptism of the Holy Spirit" is mentioned six times in the New Testament, and five of those times refer to John's prediction.[1] Obviously John was predicting the outpouring of the Holy Spirit on the day of Pentecost, which occurred a few years later (Acts 2:1–4). The "baptism of fire" is more difficult to interpret. Was it synonymous with Holy Spirit baptism? Or was it a reference to a judgment on those who would not be followers of Christ? Or was it something else?

The Old Testament prophet Joel predicted fire from God would be revealed in a supernatural way in the last days (Joel 2:30). In Peter's sermon at Pentecost, he referenced Joel's prophecy and said it was fulfilled by the outpouring of the Holy Spirit on the day of Pentecost (Acts 2:19). John seemed to view the baptism of fire in the context of a final judgment which was to begin with the ministry of Jesus and was brought to light at Pentecost (Matt. 3:11–12).

The Baptism of Jesus

The baptism of Jesus initiated Jesus' public ministry and, in one sense, was the conclusion of John's. John had never backed away from preaching his message or demanding a response from anyone. Average people (v. 5), religious leaders

(v. 7), and political figures were targets of his fiery sermons (Luke 3:19), but he was stunned in the presence of Jesus of Nazareth. John recognized his own sin and initially balked at the idea of baptizing Jesus. Instead, he desired to be baptized by Jesus (vv. 13–14). He relented, of course, because Jesus insisted that together they would "fulfill all righteousness." John baptized Jesus, therefore, because Jesus said it was the right thing to do (v. 15).

On that remarkable day John immersed the Lord Jesus in the Jordan River (v. 16). What happened next was as indescribable as it was incredible. Heaven opened up, and the Spirit of God came down in a visible way and settled upon Jesus (v. 16). For John, his ministry as a forerunner to the Messiah was essentially complete in that moment.

Most of us would not choose the lifestyle or mission of John the Baptist. He lived his life as an austere desert dweller on the fringes of human interaction (Luke 1:80) and was ultimately arrested and executed while still a young man (Mark 6:17–28). He found joy not in life's luxuries but as a servant and friend to Jesus (John 3:29). John's testimony about Jesus was profound, but perhaps his testimony about himself was equally profound and desirable for disciples today. In his exit from "the stage" of history, he said of Jesus, "He must increase, but I must decrease" (John 3:30).

For Memory and Meditation
"He must increase, but I must decrease." John 3:30

---

[1] Craig L. Blomberg, *Matthew*, vol. 22, The New American Commentary (Nashville: Broadman Press, 1992), 79.

The Sermon on the Mount

Focal Text: Matthew 5–7

Of all the teachings of Jesus, perhaps none is better known, more loved, or more misunderstood than the Sermon on the Mount. Anyone who has taken the Sermon and human nature seriously has experienced the frustration of not being able to fully live by its commands.

The Sermon on the Mount is demanding, yet it is the message of Jesus to His followers and portrays a life which can be lived when a personal relationship with Christ is present. The pastoral scholarship of John R. W. Stott is helpful at this point. He writes: "For the standards of the Sermon are neither readily attainable by every man, nor totally unattainable by any man. To put them beyond anybody's reach is to ignore the purpose of Christ's Sermon; to put them within everybody's reach is to ignore the reality of man's sin. They are attainable all right, but only by those who have experienced the new birth."[1]

The Beatitudes
Matthew 5:1–12

Nine times Jesus pronounced a blessing in the introduction of the Sermon. The word *blessed* means, "oh how happy." The blessings, however, appear at first to be anything but a cause for happiness. His kingdom operates in a counterintuitive way where being poor in spirit, mournful, meek, persecuted, and insulted (vv. 3–5, 10–11) are badges of honor. Most of us can relate to the desirability of being merciful, pure in heart, and

17

willing to make peace (vv.7–9), even if our own agendas often get in the way, but insults and persecutions (v. 11) are another story.

The blessings promised are clear. We inherit the kingdom, find comfort, inherit the earth, discover righteousness and mercy, see God, and are called the sons of God (vv. 3–9). In every case the blessings of His kingdom are spiritual in nature rather than physical or political. For instance, the blessing is not to be poor in spirit, but instead it is in receiving the kingdom of heaven (v. 3). The blessing is not being pure in heart, even though that is a blessing in itself; the blessing is seeing God as a result (v. 8). In the same way, almost all of the blessings Jesus promised, while preceded by actions in this life (being merciful, making peace, remaining pure, etc.) are realized in another world. He leads us to long for the kingdom of heaven (vv. 3, 10), to see God (v. 8), to be called sons of God (v. 9), and to find our reward in heaven (v. 12).

In addition, Jesus fully anticipated the challenges His followers would face. He promised a life of insult, which means being disgraced, persecution, a word which means to be pursued by a predator, and being lied about in every conceivable way simply because we follow Christ (v. 11). Yes, Jesus promised blessings, but they are not the kind people usually hope to receive. His blessings demonstrate that Jesus is much more than a philosopher who merely advocated a new kind of civility; instead, His blessings look beyond this life.

Salt, Light, and the Word
Matthew 5:13–20

Immediately after identifying the blessings of His kingdom, Jesus defined His followers using two metaphors: salt and light

(vv. 13–14). Salt was common in Jesus' day and was mined from the water and hills around the Dead Sea.

The second metaphor describing His followers, light, is a common theme in Scripture and is found more than 220 times in more than two hundred verses in the English text. Interestingly, the creation of light is the first thing God "says" in Scripture (Gen. 1:3) and the first thing He declared to be "good" (Gen. 1:4). Both of these metaphors describe something that cannot be denied once it is introduced (salt to the taste and light to the eyes), and the use of the definite article ("the salt"/"the light") indicates the unique role of the church in the world. Each of the properties can lose their effectiveness, however, and therefore Jesus warns that the value of the church can be compromised.

After announcing an ethical description of His disciples' role in the world, Jesus turned to the standard by which disciples can hope to be salt and light in a decadent and dark world. The rule by which we live is the Word of God (vv. 17–18). Jesus advocated for an authority of Scripture, which reaches to "the smallest letter or stroke" (v. 18). It will be difficult to find a stronger argument for the grammatical inerrancy of Scripture anywhere more convincing than from the words of the Lord Himself in this passage. Since the Word of God is eternal, outlasting both heaven and earth (v. 18) and true in the smallest detail, disciples can do with confidence exactly what Jesus instructed.

Relationships
Matthew 5:21–47

In the next section of the Sermon, Jesus moved to a description of relationships in His kingdom. In six verses Jesus refers to what His hearers had previously been taught regarding a range of common relational issues (vv. 21, 27, 31, 33, 38, 43). In six other verses He compared those common interpretations to what "I say to you" (vv. 22, 27, 32, 34, 39, 44), thus indicating His incredible sense of personal authority. In each of the six examples, Jesus went beyond the strictest interpretations of Old Testament regulations.

The law said, "You shall not commit murder" (v. 21), but Jesus said not to be unmercifully angry (vv. 22–26). The law said, "You shall not commit adultery" (v. 27), but Jesus said not to entertain private lustful thoughts (vv. 28–30). He narrowed the reason for divorce and showed much more concern for the wife (vv. 31–32). Previously there were regulations for making oaths to God, but Jesus said not to make them at all (vv. 33–37). At one time people could exact revenge, but Jesus said to turn the other cheek (vv. 38–42). Other teachers said, "You shall love your neighbor," but Jesus said we should love our enemies (vv. 43–48). Clearly Jesus called His followers to demanding standards exceeding previous expectations.

Spiritual Life
Matthew 6:1–24

In Jesus' time people engaged in three common expressions of spiritual devotion—giving offerings to the poor, prayer, and fasting. Jesus turned His attention to these three with a particular focus on hypocrisy and authenticity. The discussion of the three actions follows a pattern. In each case Jesus advocates for these practices if they are not practiced like the "hypocrites" (vv. 2, 5, 16) and if they are done in "secret" (vv. 4, 6, 18). Of the three practices, prayer will get much more discussion and attention in the rest of the New Testament than the other two. All of the New Testament writers taught on prayer overtly, in hundreds of verses, in almost all of the books. It is not surprising that the first teaching on prayer in the New Testament came from the Lord Himself in the Sermon on the Mount (vv. 5–8). His "school of prayer" included the most famous prayer of all time, "the Lord's Prayer," in which Jesus essentially gave His followers a prayer guide (vv. 9–13).

Treasure and Worry
Matthew 6:19–34

In this section Jesus contrasts our obsession with things over against eternal values. He highlights this struggle by pointing out two treasures, two visions (one light and the other dark) and two masters (vv. 19–24). He then uses the common needs of every life—food, water and clothing—and familiar illustrations from common experience (wild birds and wild flowers), to show how worry (a word which comes from the Greek word meaning "to be divided") distracts us from trusting God (vv. 25–32).

Jesus never denies the needs of humanity; on the contrary He acknowledges that God knows we "need" these things (v. 32). Instead of minimizing our physical reality, Jesus points us to a greater pursuit in life. He argues that each of us should "seek first" the kingdom of God. The word *seek* is an imperative verb with the force of a command. The word *first* is the Greek word *protos* (from which we get words like *prototype*) and means "first in importance." In other words, the life of the follower of Jesus is not primarily a pursuit of material securities but, instead, is the pursuit of God's rule and provision over all of life. In one of the most important verses in the New Testament, Jesus urges us to pursue God's reign and trust in His riches (v. 33).

Judging Others
Matthew 7:1–5

Jesus said, "Do not judge" (v. 1) and then offered an exaggerated illustration to clarify His point. He reminded His followers to remove the "log" in their own eye (v. 3) so that they might see clearly to remove "a speck" from a brother's eye. Only after dealing with our own failures are we in a position to deal with the failings of others. Clearly there are times to exercise judgment ("then you will see clearly to take the speck out of your brother's eye") but only when we are clean of the same issues (v. 5). Any other approach is hypocritical (v. 5).

Persistent Prayer
Matthew 7:7–11

Jesus returned to the subject of prayer to insist that His followers persist in prayer. He uses three synonyms for prayer—"ask," "seek," and "knock" (vv. 7–8)—to assure His followers that under certain conditions we might expect prayer to be answered. Each of the three verbs is in the present tense suggesting the continuous action of asking, seeking, and knocking. He then illustrated the willingness of God to answer favorably by comparing and contrasting Him to a loving human father who wants to give what his children ask rather than outrageous substitutes such as a snake instead of a fish or a stone in place of a loaf of bread (vv. 9–11).

Doing Good
Matthew 7:12

In one of His most famous sayings often referred to as "the Golden Rule," Jesus places the impetus of social behavior upon His followers rather than upon those they encounter. He said we should anticipate how we would want to be treated and initiate that kind of action toward others. In relationships we have to act first to do right. He would later say something equivalent when He was asked about ranking commandments in order of their importance. He said, "Love your neighbor as yourself" (Matt. 22:39). In both instances He said these are summaries of the Old Testament law (7:12; 22:40).

Final Judgment
Matthew 7:13–29

In the last section of the Sermon, Jesus uses three examples to warn His followers. He mentions two gates, two fruit trees, and two foundations. Each of these illustrates the final analysis of life. The wide gate opens itself to final destruction while the narrow gate is life for the few who find it (vv. 13–14). The bad tree is cut down while the good tree produces a fruit easily recognized and favored (vv. 15–23). The house built on the foundation of sand, representing those who ignore the words of Jesus (v. 26), is washed away (v. 27). The house built on a rock foundation, however, survives the storms and the floods and describes the person who obeys the words of Jesus (vv. 24–25).

The Authority of Jesus
Matthew 7:28–29

The teachings of Jesus were like nothing His followers had ever heard. The word *amazed* (v. 28) literally means they were "struck out" of their senses. In our vernacular we might say they were "knocked out" or "blown away" by what they heard. What other teacher would dare conclude that one's eternal destiny would be determined by the response to His teachings (vv. 21–23, 24–26)?

Today Jesus' words are as controversial and unique as they were back then. His message is as radical as it ever was, and His authority has not been diminished. Jesus still teaches that our eternal destiny depends on what we do in response to Him.

For Memory and Meditation

"Blessed are the pure in heart, for they shall see God." Matthew 5:8

---

[1] John R. W. Stott, *The Message of the Sermon on the Mount*, The Bible Speaks Today (Downers Grove, IL: IVP Academic, 1993), 29.

Who Is Jesus?

Focal Text: Matthew 16:13–20

Has there ever been anyone like Jesus of Nazareth? Who has ever had more followers? Who has ever been more loved? More books have been written about Him than about any other figure in history. He has hundreds of millions of followers today and has been the subject of art, poetry, music, speculation, adoration, misrepresentation, and drama for two thousand years. Academicians, politicians, athletes, entertainers, authors, skeptics, and people from almost every walk of life have passionate opinions about Jesus.

Yet, in spite of Jesus' worldwide influence, recognition, and popularity, for about two hundred years scholars have been "searching" for the "historic" Jesus as if no generation has yet comprehended Him. Perhaps none ever has. The sheer volume of scholastic information and popular speculation about Jesus is almost overwhelming, adding a greater degree of intrigue to one of His most pointed questions, "Who do you say that I am?" (Matt. 16:15). His question deserves an answer. Who is Jesus?

Caesarea Philippi
Matthew 16:13

Jesus had traveled with His disciples approximately twenty-five miles north of the Sea of Galilee to retreat for prayer and to prepare His disciples for His death on the cross. In Luke's Gospel we learn one of the most important reasons for the spiritual retreat. "While He was praying alone, the disciples were with Him, and He questioned them, saying, 'Who do the people say that I am?'" (Luke 9:18). Jesus had already attempted to withdraw for prayer and perhaps to train His small group of disciples, but the crowds around the Sea of Galilee were demanding, and Jesus found it increasingly difficult to find time alone.

A review of the activities leading up to His retreat to Caesarea Philippi makes His reasons for the retreat more obvious. He had recently and miraculously fed crowds of several thousand on two separate occasions (Matt. 14:13–21; 15:29–39). In both instances Jesus appears to have been attempting to get away for spiritual reflection and physical rest, and probably for more intensive training of His disciples, but the miracles of feeding the thousands were interruptions to His plans (Matt. 14:13; 15:29–30). These miraculous events put Him in even more demand around the Sea of Galilee where His ministry was located so He finally headed north to Caesarea Philippi.

Caesarea Philippi was a non-Jewish region where Jesus could find the privacy that had eluded Him in Galilee. It was a center for pagan worship where at various times in history Baal worship with its human sacrifices had been practiced. Later the mythological half man-half goat fertility god Pan was worshipped there. In fact, the name of the area before Jesus' time was Panias, similar to its contemporary local name, Banias. The infamous Herod the Great had erected a solid white marble temple to worship Caesar there, and his son Herod Philip the tetrarch (a governor of a quarter) had renamed the area Caesarea Philippi in honor of Caesar and himself. In short, the area was a pluralistic convergence of ancient and contemporary religion, paganism, politics, and philosophy, but there the greatest confession of faith in the New Testament so far would be declared.

The Son of Man
Matthew 16:13

In the reflective and beautiful setting of Caesarea Philippi, at the headwaters of the Jordan River, Jesus posed a question to His disciples about the common opinion of the Son of Man. Both Mark and Luke use the personal pronoun "I" in place of the title "Son of Man" (Mark 8:27; Luke 9:18), leaving no doubt about whom Jesus meant by "Son of Man." The title is used repeatedly in the Synoptic Gospels to describe Jesus but, interestingly, only by Jesus Himself (Matt. 8:20; 9:6; 10:23; 11:19; 12:8; Mark 14:41; 14:62; Luke 5:24; 6:22; etc.).

The title comes from the Old Testament prophecy of Daniel where he saw "one like a Son of Man was coming, and He came up to the Ancient of Days and was presented before Him. And to Him was given dominion, glory and a kingdom, that all the peoples, nations and men of every language might serve Him. His dominion is an everlasting dominion which will not pass away; and His kingdom is one which will not be destroyed" (Dan. 7:13–14). Obviously Jesus knew that His first hearers were familiar with the prophecy concerning the "Son of Man," and His insistence upon applying it to Himself in the presence of disciples, crowds, and even enemies raises the question for us that Jesus would pose next: Who is Jesus? Who else in his right mind would consistently apply to himself a title so grandiose if he were not the one predicted? Only Jesus could refer to Himself as the One with "a kingdom . . . which will not be destroyed" and "an everlasting dominion which will not pass away." When a man sees Himself in those terms, it is a fair question to ask, as the disciples had done in the early days of His ministry, "Who then is this, that even the wind and the sea obey Him?" (Mark 4:41).

What the Crowds Were Saying
Matthew 16:13–14

Jesus asked His disciples what others were saying about Him, and they were ready with answers regarding the popular conclusions of the day. They listed four options: John the Baptist, Elijah, Jeremiah, and finally the vague description, "one of the prophets." Herod had expressed the idea that Jesus was John the Baptist "risen from the dead" (Matt. 14:2). Herod had executed John, and his conscience, like a scene from Edgar Allen Poe's "Tell-Tale Heart," was bothering him.

The other answers given, "Elijah; . . . Jeremiah, or one of the prophets," reflected both the excitement and the confusion regarding Jesus' public and misunderstood ministry. Each of the speculations, while meant perhaps in a complimentary way (they were certainly better than the conclusions of the Pharisees who said He was "Beelzebub the ruler of the demons" [Matt. 10:25; 12:24]), were, nevertheless, insufficient. Jesus was not just one more in a long line of godly representatives. His true identity, like His self-designation, "Son of Man," demands much more consideration than merely lumping Him among even a stellar group of previous religious leaders.

The Confession of the Disciples
Matthew 16:15–17

From the beginning of His public ministry, Jesus had attracted followers. Many of these were superficial and retracted their allegiance when the demands of following Him were deemed by them to be too great (John 6:66). Some of them, however, remained loyal to Him and eventually would become His ambassadors to the world. Chief among those in the early days was Simon, whom Jesus renamed Peter (Matt. 16:16).

Simon Peter was a commercial fisherman on the Sea of Galilee in a partnership with his brother Andrew and two other men who became disciples of Jesus, James and John (Matt. 18–20; Luke 5:10). He had what appears to be a lucrative business with several employees (Mark 1:16–20) and vocally wondered about the practical consequences of giving up not only his business but all of his possessions (Matt. 19:27). He was originally from Bethsaida, a fishing village on the northeast corner of the Sea of Galilee, but he maintained a home in the more prominent city of Capernaum on the northwest corner of the lake (Mark 1:29). He was married (1 Cor. 9:5), and his mother-in- law was still living when he met Jesus. She became one of the first recipients of Jesus' healing ministry (Mark 1:30–31).

Simon Peter was frequently the spokesman on behalf of the other disciples (Matt. 15:15; Luke 12:41; etc.) when Jesus was addressing all of them. The question at Caesarea Philippi was no exception. Jesus turned to His small group of intimate friends and asked, "Who do you say that I am?" The "you" in His question is plural. He asked it of the group. Simon Peter did not wait for a consensus. He almost blurted out, "You are the Christ, the Son of the living God" (Matt. 16:16). This is the first time in His ministry anyone had called Jesus "the Christ."

The word *Christ* comes from the Greek word *Christos*, which means "to anoint." In the Old Testament it is used as the means of conferring authority upon the King. While sometimes used to describe anointing for priests (Exod. 28:41; etc.), of the near- ly seventy times the word is used in the Old Testament, most examples refer to anointing the king with oil, poured upon his head from a horn (1 Sam. 10:1; 1 Sam. 16:12–13; 1 Kings 1:39). When David was anointed by Samuel the prophet, the Holy Spirit came upon him with power (1 Sam. 16:13). Therefore the Jewish people saw "anointing" as a necessary spiritual bestowal of God's authority upon His chosen servant.

In the New Testament the term *Christ* is used more than five hundred times as the title for Jesus of Nazareth, the "Son of the living God" (Matt. 16:16). Jesus had referred to Himself as the "Son of Man," but Peter called Him the "Son of God." Rather than reject Peter's praise as overstatement, Jesus blessed Peter and reminded him that the revelation of Christ is never discovered by human intellect, investigation, or intuition. Instead, it is a matter of spiritual illumination (v. 17).

The Church on the Rock
Matthew 16:18–20

Jesus responded to Peter by acknowledging that the confession was correct. What He said next has been a source of doctrinal debate for centuries. He said, "You are Peter (the Greek word *petros*), and upon this rock (*petra*) I will build My church." Catholic dogma says Peter was the first pope and cites this as one text in defense of that position. Since at least the Reformation, some Protestants have argued that the "rock" upon which the church was to be built is the confession of Peter, namely, "You are the Christ," not Peter himself. The text does not anticipate a papacy, or an ecclesiology fitting the Roman Catholic Church (or any other church structure for that matter). In fact, this is the first of only three times Jesus mentions the church in the book of Matthew (Matt. 18:17 mentions the church twice). Peter would later see all believers like "living stones . . . being built up as a spiritual house" (1 Pet. 2:5), perhaps expanding on the theme of Jesus. The church belongs to Jesus, but it is made up of people.

Peter did go on to lead the early church, representing the other apostles as the main preacher at Pentecost (Acts 2:14–

40), leading the effort to win Gentiles (Acts 10:23–48), and deciding the outcome of the first church council (Acts 15:6–11). In addition, Paul acknowledged that the church was "built on the foundation of the apostles and prophets, Christ Jesus Himself being the corner stone" (Eph. 2:20). In this sense Peter, along with all of the apostles and several other key figures in the early movement, played a strategic role in the development of the church. So the church is built on a confession that Jesus is the Christ (see also Phil. 2:10–11) and upon the leaders called by the Lord.

Regardless of other appointed leaders, however, the church belongs to Jesus. It is His church. He will build it, and it will rest on a foundation of His choosing, which He regards as solid. In addition, He said, "The gates of Hades will not overpower it." Hades (translated "hell" in ESV, KJV) in the New Testament is the realm of the dead and describes the place where the wicked are in conscious torment (Luke 16:23; Rev. 20:14). The "gates of Sheol [Hades]" is an idiomatic expression referring to death (Isa. 38:10), and Jesus was declaring that His church is alive and will outlast even the powers of death and hell.

Binding and Loosing
Matthew 16:19–20

Jesus did not hand Peter a literal ring of keys but instead was using metaphorical and picturesque language to teach about the authority of the disciples of Jesus. As when reading all metaphors, we must take care not to push the imagery farther than the speaker intended. Keys open and close gates and doors, and whoever controls the keys has authority. While Jesus was speaking directly to Peter in this instance, Peter was acting as a spokesman for all of the disciples to whom Jesus had originally addressed the questions that led to the current exchange between Jesus and Simon Peter (see Matt. 18:18 where Jesus said all of the disciples have authority for "binding and loosing").

The question is, what did Jesus mean by "binding and loosing"? The image of the keys suggests the ability to open the doors to the kingdom of God. Binding and loosing must relate to the locked or unlocked gates. The phrase "binding and loosing" was familiar among the rabbis as a way of describing what was "permissible" and "unallowable" for the faithful, based on the interpretation of Scripture.[1] Did Peter not do just that, along with the other disciples on the day of Pentecost (Acts 2:14–41), by interpreting the cross and the resurrection of Jesus to the thousands assembled to hear the sermon? His conclusion that day would be exactly the same as at Caesarea Philippi. He preached, "God has made Him both Lord and Christ" (Acts 2:36). He thus tutored every future witness how to use the "keys" to invite people into the kingdom.

The tense of the participles *bound* and *loosed* describes action completed in the past, not needing to be repeated. Therefore Jesus was saying, "Whatever you bind on earth will *have already been bound in heaven*" (author's translation). In other words, the preachers, teachers, and witnesses of Jesus who interpret Him to the world are "binding and loosing" what is already done in heaven. Heaven does not ratify our actions; it precedes them.

Jesus concluded the lessons of the retreat by urging the disciples not to tell anyone that He was the Christ. There would be an appropriate time for that, but as the rest of Matthew demonstrates, they had much more to learn about what it means that Jesus is the Christ (see v. 21).

For Memory and Meditation

"He said to them, 'But who do you say that I am?' Simon Peter answered, 'You are the Christ, the Son of the living God.'" Matthew 16:15–16

---

[1] Michael Green, *The Message of Matthew* (Leicester, England: Inter-Varsity Press, 1988), 180.

The Last Days of Jesus

Focal Text: Matthew 21–25

When the story of Jesus' life was written, large sections of His life were deliberately left absent. John said that if everything Jesus said and did had been recorded, "the whole world would not have room for the books" (John 21:25). Clearly the Gospel writers had plenty of material to choose from; but, guided by the Holy Spirit, they carefully chose those events from the life of Jesus that best communicated their intended message. Therefore, little from the life of Christ can be found in all four Gospels.

Two of the Gospels, for example, ignore everything about His birth and childhood. The last week of His life, however, was so important that His four biographers spent more than 25 percent of their accounts describing it in analytical detail.

Consider for instance the Gospel of Matthew. He devotes about 36 percent of the 1,066 verses of his story to only the last six days of Jesus' life and the weekend that followed. The other three Gospels are similar. Can you imagine reading a biography of any other historical figures and discovering that nothing is said of 90 percent of their lives, while a third of the book details only the last week of their lives?

Obviously, Jesus' last days preoccupied the attention of His biographers. Someone once observed that "the Gospels . . . are chronicles of Jesus' final week with increasingly longer introductions."[1]

Several of His most severe pronouncements of judgment (Matt. 23:1–36) and direct confrontations with critics took place during His last week. Much could be said about these subjects, but in order to get a broad grasp of the importance of Jesus' last days, four specific events in the days before the cross must be highlighted.

The Triumphal Entry
Matthew 21:1–11

As he did in the birth narrative at the beginning of his Gospel, Matthew is careful in the story of the triumphal entry to link the event to the messianic prophecies of the Old Testament. The entry of Jesus into the city electrified the hopes of the populace and terrified the religious leaders. This was a fulfillment of Zechariah 9:9–10 where the prophet looks forward to the King of the Jews "just and endowed with salvation, humble and mounted on a donkey, even on a colt, the foal of a donkey." That scene, complete with the rejoicing of the people, was being spontaneously played out as Jesus rode into Jerusalem.

Matthew does not mention any of Jesus' previous visits to Jerusalem although the other Gospel writers do (Luke 2:21–49; John 2:13; 5:1; 7:14; etc.), so the drama of His final entry is intensified. As Jesus rode down the Mount of Olives toward the city of Jerusalem, the crowds, present for the Passover celebrations, erupted in praise (21:9–10) quoting Scripture and singing "hosanna to the Son of David" (v. 9). The title "Son of David" was a messianic reference, and the Hebrew word *hosanna* literally means "save, I pray."

Matthew opened his Gospel with the story of magi coming into the city of Jerusalem with a question, "Where is He who has been born King of the Jews?" (Matt. 2:2). Now in the conclusion of the Gospel, the answer is clear. The King of the Jews had entered the Holy City, and the long overdue coronation parade was finally occurring. The joy of that moment wouldn't last long, but events that followed would confirm that the King had indeed arrived.

The Cleansing of the Temple
Matthew 21:12–17

The Old Testament ended with a warning about the severity of One who would suddenly come to the temple with "a refiner's fire" (Mal. 3:2). Jesus embodied that image as He reminded those standing nearby that the temple was to be a "house of prayer" rather than "a robbers' den" (Matt. 21:13), a statement which combined two Old Testament references (Isa. 56:7; Jer. 7:11). Clearly Jesus was contrasting the importance of pure worship to the crass spectacle He found that day.

The cleansing of the temple occurred in the court of the Gentiles, which was designed to allow Gentiles the opportunity to worship the one true God of Israel. The Jewish religious leaders advocated the practice of selling animals worthy of sacrifice and a currency exchange for coins acceptable for the temple tax. While it is hard to argue with the motivation behind allowing these practices, given Judaism's insistence on ritual purity and the importance of unblemished sacrifices on God's altar (Mal. 1:7–14), the concept of worship and prayer had been lost in the clamor of commerce in the area intended for prayer.

By driving out the vendors and turning over their tables, Jesus was exercising an authority over all the Jewish leaders, the worshippers, and the temple itself. To make that clear, Jesus performed the only healing miracles in the temple recorded in the New Testament. Both the blind and the lame came to Jesus, and He healed them, demonstrating that He would fulfill the hopes of the "house of prayer." Isaiah had promised that even those as previously unwelcome as "eunuchs" and "foreigners" could worship God in the house of prayer (Isa. 56:3–7). The miracles of Jesus indicate that the disenfranchised had found a Savior!

Even children were bursting into songs of praise to Jesus, praise which belonged to Yahweh alone, incurring the anger of the religious authorities (Matt. 21:15–16). Whatever control the Jewish leaders had previously exercised over the temple precincts was lost in the events of that day. Jesus was the indisputable Lord of the temple of God.

The Great Commandment
Matthew 22:34–40

In the Gospels the two distinct provocateurs against Jesus from the Jewish ranks were the Pharisees and the Sadducees. Usually at odds with each other as groups with different theological and philosophical outlooks, they were aligned in a common opposition against Jesus.

When the Pharisees heard that Jesus had easily dismissed the criticisms of the Sadducees (the root word used by Matthew in verse 34 is from the verb "to muzzle"), they were anxious to give their debate skills a try. No doubt they had argued among themselves countless times about the greatest commandment. Some have suggested that the Pharisees turned Judaism from a religion of sacrifice to a religion of "law."[2] They had discovered more than six hundred commandments divided into categories regarding who had to obey, when, and where. Vigorous theological debates likely swirled among them about which were the most important commandments and why.

So they assumed Jesus could not satisfactorily answer a question that had tied them into theological knots. They were wrong. Jesus said the greatest commandment is to love God with everything we have—heart, soul, and mind. Who could argue with that? Hadn't God said the same thing through Moses (Deut. 6:5)? Both Pharisees and Sadducees could agree with the instruction of the law! Jesus preemptively added the second greatest commandment as well. We must love our neighbor. Again all the Jews had to agree. It was instructed in the law (Lev. 19:18). Apparently no teacher before had ever used these two Old Testament instructions together. Jesus did not say these are the only commandments, but He did say they are the greatest.

The Olivet Discourse
Matthew 24–25
The Bible is a book full of prophecy. It should be no surprise, therefore, that Jesus predicted the future. One day His disciples were admiring the temple, but Jesus reminded them a day was coming when the temple would be destroyed. Jesus then described the most sweeping prophecy of future events found anywhere in the New Testament outside the book of Revelation. The following section is an overview of His vision.

Birth Pangs (24:1–8)
Jesus described a period of history that would be characterized by false Christs, international conflict, and natural disasters. He called this period the time of birth pangs. Jesus made clear that these signs do not typify "the end" but rather they are the birth pangs that grow more frequent and more intense as the labor nears birth.

39

Persecution and Evangelization (24:9–14)

The time before the end sounds terrible for followers of Christ. Persecutions, imprisonment, and martyrdom are all assured. Yet in the midst of these horrors, the preaching (the Greek word means "to publicly proclaim") of the gospel will reach the nations of the world. The worldwide evangelistic thrust is the last sign before "the end."

Great Tribulation (24:15–28)

In verse 14, Jesus said, "Then the end will come." In verse 15, however, He returns with much more informing detail that will occur prior to the end.

Jesus predicted a time for the world that will be so bad, unless God intervenes, "no life would have been saved" (v. 22). He called that period "a great tribulation" ("distress," v. 21, NIV). This time appears to be the last days of history. The word *distress* comes from a Greek word meaning "to press" and describes the forces of external pressure. Jesus warned that the world has never seen so horrendous a time and never will again (v. 21).

The Appearance of Christ (24:29–31)

Jesus said that immediately after the time of distress, the sun and moon will experience an apparent cosmological event that would presumably end life on earth (v. 29). During this event the Lord Himself will appear in the sky, and people everywhere will see Him even as the "elect" will be gathered together by angelic forces (v. 30).

An Unknown Hour (24:32–39)

Using analogies from nature and Scripture, Jesus insisted

that the sudden appearance of "the Son of Man" will come at an unknown time. Even He did not know when that end-time event will occur (v. 36).

The Sudden Disappearance (24:40–44)

At some point in the unfolding drama of end-time events, people will suddenly disappear from otherwise normal activities. Two men will be in a field working; two women will be preparing grain for a meal when without warning one person from each scene is supernaturally "taken" while the other is "left" (vv. 40–41). Since Jesus has already described His visible appearance, and the dramatic solar and stellar disruptions that follow a great tribulation in which no one can survive (vv. 22, 29), the sudden disappearance of people from view cannot follow those events in a chronological sequence. The sudden disappearance of people from the earth sounds like Paul's description of being "caught up together with them in the clouds to meet the Lord in the air" (1 Thess. 4:17).

The rest of the Olivet Discourse urges disciples to be constantly vigilant while waiting for the return of Christ and a final judgment (vv. 42–51; 25:1–46). Jesus uses vivid parables describing the sudden appearance of a bridegroom (Matt. 25:1–13) and a traveling property owner (Matt. 25:14–30) to insist on constant readiness for those who wait for His return.

Conclusion

The last days of Jesus were some of the most dramatic and productive of His life. Much of what we know of the Christian life was made most clear in the hours before the cross. No wonder the Gospel writers moved so deliberately and carefully through the events of the last days of Jesus.

For Memory and Meditation

"And He said to him, 'You shall love the Lord your God with all your heart, and with all your soul, and with all your mind.' This is the great and foremost commandment. The second is like it, 'You shall love your neighbor as yourself.'" Matthew 22:37–39

---

[1] Phillip Yancey, *The Jesus I Never Knew* (Grand Rapids, MI: Zondervan Press, 1995), 187.

[2] Clayton Harrop and Charles W Draper, *Holman Illustrated Bible Dictionary* (Nashville: Holman Bible Publishers, 2003), 917.

The Cross of Jesus

Focal Text: Matthew 26–27

The most significant event in history was the crucifixion of Jesus. Many years ago Billy Graham wrote, "The heart of the Christian Gospel with its incarnation and atonement is in the cross and the resurrection. Jesus was born to die."[1] Every person ever born will die, but Jesus was born to die! Why? In the brutality of the crucifixion, we discover the problem of human sin, the need for a Savior, and the good news of eternal salvation.

The Betrayal
Matthew 26:14–15

Every mention of Judas Iscariot in the New Testament places him at the end of the list of the twelve apostles and includes some negative reference (Matt. 10:4; Mark 3:19; Luke 6:16; John 12:4–6; etc.). The New Testament writers left no ambiguity about his character or his role in the death of Jesus. Judas was a thief, a betrayer, controlled by Satan, and after death he went "where he belongs" (Acts 1:25, NIV).

The Gospel writers established the fact that Jesus was completely innocent and did not deserve the betrayal of Judas. The death of Jesus, from a human perspective, was the ultimate injustice. The "thirty pieces of silver" (v. 15) represented probably no more than six months' wages for the common worker of Jesus' day. It is inconceivable that Judas could betray Jesus for any price, let alone so paltry a sum. The betrayer embodies the old adage, "He knew the price of everything and the value of nothing."

The Last Supper
Matthew 26:17–30

Every believer today is familiar with the Lord's Supper or Communion. Jesus took a common Jewish practice and infused it with a new meaning related to His impending death on the cross.

Originally the Jews celebrated the meal as "the Passover" (v. 17), commemorating the escape of Moses and the Israelite slaves out of Egypt. The meal looked back to the blood of a sacrificial lamb smeared onto "the two doorposts and on the lintel of the houses" (Exod. 12:7). This gesture alerted the death angel to pass over that home so that the plague of the death of the firstborn would not touch the home protected by the blood (Exod. 12:13).

The Passover was also a time of eating unleavened bread to remind the participants that the Israelites left Egypt in haste before the bread could rise (Exod. 23:15). Therefore, the Passover is also referred to as the Feast of Unleavened Bread.

Jesus took the two common elements of the Passover and focused not on the exodus but instead on His own death. Jesus called the bread "My body" (Matt. 26:26). He then referred to the cup of the evening meal as "My blood of the covenant, which is poured out for many for forgiveness of sins" (Matt. 26:28).

Who else but the Son of God could reassign the meaning of a festival of worship designed and commanded by God Himself? Jesus was more than a preacher or prophet. Jesus made clear that all previous sacrifices pointed to His final sacrifice for sin, once and for all. His death on the cross would now be the focal point of our worship toward God.

Gethsemane
Matthew 26:36–46

After the Last Supper Jesus and His disciples retired to the garden of Gethsemane on the eastern slope of the Mount of Olives. Once there Jesus separated His followers into two groups, inviting three of His men to pray with Him. Then Jesus confided His emotional turmoil. He described being "deeply grieved, to the point of death" (Matt. 26:38). He asked them to stay nearby and pray as He suffered with the reality that He would soon die a brutal death on the cross. Unfortunately the disciples fell asleep. While they slept, Jesus prayed for deliverance, if it could be God's will, from the "cup" (vv. 39, 42, 44). Jesus had already used the metaphor of a cup to describe suffering (Matt. 20:22), and it is obvious from His emotional prayer that the "cup" mentioned in His Gethsemane prayer is none other than "the horrifying cup of vicarious suffering."[2] Obviously Jesus foresaw the horror of the cross, and yet He was completely yielded to the inevitability of the cross as the will of God for His life (vv. 39, 42, 44).

The Arrest
Matthew 26:47–56

The quiet scene of the garden prayer meeting changed dramatically when a large crowd of soldiers (John 18:3) and officers from the Jewish leaders, armed with swords and clubs, stormed into Gethsemane ready to arrest Jesus. Judas was their leader and famously identified Jesus by kissing Him. The

45

mood was tense and violent, demonstrated by one of the disciples (identified as Peter in John 18:10) drawing a sword and lunging at the head of one of the men, cutting off his ear. In the midst of the confusion and chaos of the moment, Jesus was remarkably unflustered. In fact, His concern was elsewhere. Rather than fretting about the mob surrounding Him, Jesus was instead only focused on the mission of the cross, insisting that the apparent horror unfolding was all part of God's plan revealed in Scripture (Matt. 26:54, 56).

The Trial
Matthew 26:57–68

Like the other events immediately surrounding the crucifixion of Jesus, the theme that emerges from the makeshift trial is obvious: the action is marching the reader toward the cross. Matthew wastes no time indicting the Sanhedrin. He reminds us that they could only bring "false testimony" (v. 59) and that the Sanhedrin was not interested in justice but were only looking for a way to "put Him to death" (v. 59). Far from being unsettled or anxious, Jesus was the pillar of strength and poise. He knew His appointed time had arrived, and He was already looking beyond the cross to the glory of sitting "at the right hand of Power" (v. 64). At no time does the New Testament portray Jesus as a victim of the religious or political pressures of His day. Instead, He is seen as the One who anticipates the cross and sees it as God's perfect will for His life.

Jesus before Pilate
Matthew 27:11–25

When Jesus stood before Pilate, the Roman governor, He astounded the Roman official with His calm and His unwillingness to defend Himself against the false charges of the chief priests. Matthew spends little time analyzing the meeting between Jesus and Pilate. After a brief meeting Pilate led Jesus out to a crowd for a question that still confronts people today. He asked, "What shall I do with Jesus who is called Christ?" (v. 22). The answer was quick in coming and completely in keeping with the Gospel's emphasis: "Crucify Him!" (v. 22) "Why?" Pilate inquires, "What evil has He done?" But legal certainties were irrelevant by now; the purpose for which Jesus had been born was unfolding faster than anyone could control. The crowd merely shouted louder. The words still echo across the centuries, "Crucify Him!" (v. 23).

The Cross
Matthew 27:26–54

The inhumanity of crucifixion would now be on full display. Pilate had ordered that Jesus was to be flogged, a word meaning to flagellate. It was a brutal torture that sometimes led to death. The victim was stripped, bound, and bent forward over a pillar or post while professional masochists administered the unthinkable beating. The whip, or the flagellum, was made of long, heavy leather strips weighted with pieces of bone or metal, which chewed away the flesh of the poor victim with each lash. Jesus' body was lacerated to the rib cage following the scourging, and the shock and blood loss could have been lethal (v. 26).

The heartless and mindless contempt of the soldiers added further pain and suffering, not to mention deeper humiliation and degradation. The Praetorian was the official residence of the Roman governor and also housed the barracks for the soldiers. There the soldiers ridiculed the beaten and bloody man's reputation as a King. They wrapped a robe around Him and forced the stinging crown of thorns upon His head. With the soldiers bowing before Him in mock allegiance, the scene grew more ominous. The men began slapping Him in the head with a hollow reed known for its sharp texture. When they could find no more pleasure in their insults, they led Him to the place of the crucifixion (vv. 27–31).

Matthew is unusually discreet, as all of the Gospel writers are, concerning the physical torture of the cross. Moviemakers, scholars, and preachers (including this author) are prone to vivid descriptions of the nails, the pain, and the blood of the cross. Interestingly, Matthew mentions none of that. He sparingly states, almost in passing, "When they had crucified Him, they divided up His garments among themselves by casting lots" (v. 35). Instead of Jesus' reaction to the crucifixion, Matthew draws our attention to the responses of those around the cross.

A recurring theme in the crucifixion narrative is contempt. For instance, His clothes are stripped from Him and made the stakes in a soldiers' game (v. 35), thus fulfilling the messianic prophecy of Psalm 22:18. Studying Psalm 22 alongside Matthew 27 reveals a pattern of prophecy and fulfillment. Matthew reminds us, "Those passing were hurling abuse at Him" (v. 39), fulfilling Psalm 22:7.

Another fulfillment of prophecy is seen in the mocking demand that Jesus should save Himself by coming down from the cross (vv. 39–44; Ps. 22:8). In fact, the thing most frequently said to Jesus while He was on the cross was a version of "save Yourself" (Mark 15:29–32; Luke 23:35–39). Generations of believers have lived with everlasting gratitude that when Jesus went to the cross He did not suffer there to save Himself but to save us.

48

The Death of Jesus
Matthew 27:45–54

Spread throughout the four canonical Gospels are "seven last words" or sayings of Jesus from the cross. The saying here in Matthew 27 is considered the fourth of these. Why did Jesus ask "why" (v. 46)? At that moment of suffering, the One who came "to seek and to save that which is lost" (Luke 19:10) is not giving up or losing hope; He is preaching an evangelistic sermon. He was pointing those nearby to the fulfillment of a well-known messianic psalm. His deeply emotional cry is a direct quotation of Psalm 22:1. The numerous religious leaders standing near Him should have instantly recognized the reference, and they would have known each prediction from the psalm. They should have seen, therefore, their own role in helping to fulfill it. Instead, they stubbornly refused to understand Jesus (vv. 47–48).

Shortly after the cry from the cross, Jesus died (v. 50). At that moment a miracle occurred. The curtain (presumably the one that separated the holy of holies from all else) was spontaneously torn from top to bottom (v. 51). God tore the curtain. The symbolism is obvious. Everyone now has access to God because of the cross.

In addition to the supernatural tearing open of the curtain, Matthew had already described a terrible, unexplainable, midday darkness covering the land while Jesus was on the cross (v. 45). A third miracle was the sudden bursting open of tombs and dead people walking out alive. The religious leaders may have tenaciously clung to their disbelief, but after seeing all He did that day, the Roman centurion on duty made a declaration of faith: "Truly this was the Son of God!" (v. 54). When we view the cross, with all of its cruelty and suffering, the centurion's conclusion should be our own. Jesus is the Son of God!

For Memory and Meditation

"Pilate said to them, 'Then what shall I do with Jesus who is called Christ?' They all said, 'Crucify Him!'" Matthew 27:22

---

[1] Billy Graham, *World Aflame* (Old Tappan, NJ: Spire Books, Fleming H. Revell, 1967), 102.

[2] R. T. France, *Matthew*, vol. 1, Tyndale New Testament Commentary (Grand Rapids, MI Wm. B. Eerdmans Publishing Co., 1987), 373.

The Resurrection and the Great Commission

Focal Text: Matthew 28

Funerals are a sad reality of life. Imagine attending the funeral of a friend and experiencing all the sadness associated with it, and then, inexplicably, that friend is publicly alive again three days later. If that miracle occurred in your life, would you tell anyone about your friend who was dead and then was alive again? Perhaps the more appropriate question is, how could you keep it quiet?

Jesus' resurrection was the miracle the early church could not keep secret. Rising from the dead validated His ministry, His authoritative teachings, His demands for discipleship, and finally, even His cross. Because He lives, the church has an urgent message of life for a dying world.

In each of the four Gospels, the authors deliberately link the resurrection of Jesus to His last instruction to the apostles. The work of proclaiming His message, preaching the gospel, is the consistent theme. This is most pronounced in Matthew (ch. 28) and Luke (ch. 24) but is also present in Mark (ch.16) and directly implied in John (ch. 21). Since Jesus defeated death, the church has work to do; we cannot be silent about our Lord's conquest over the grave. We have a story to tell.

The Angel
Matthew 28:1–7

The angel of the Lord is a familiar character in the Gospel of Matthew since the reader first encounters him in the Christmas story (1:20). Absent throughout the rest of the Gospel, the angel of the Lord returns at the time of Christ's triumph over the grave to demonstrate the power of Christ over all opposition. The earthquake that rolled the stone away from the tomb was a direct result of the angel's descent (Matt. 28:2). His appearance was terrifying, like an unexpected bolt of lightning in the darkness that startled the guards to the point of unconsciousness (v. 4). The angel's presence and actions also revealed God's power, at least subtly, by showing God's power over Rome. The mere presence of the heavenly being left the professional soldiers of the world's most feared army in a state of terrified paralysis. If the cross had been the sign of Rome's might, the appearance of the angel and the empty tomb were signs that God was in control after all.

When the guards saw the angel, they passed out "like dead men" (v. 4). It is difficult to miss the point. The guards were sent to watch a dead man, but while they were watching, He came back to life, and they appeared dead (v. 4). In any event the angel turned his attention to the women and assured them that Jesus was alive and they were to "go quickly" (v. 7) with the message. The urgency of the good news is highlighted again in the women's response as they "left . . . quickly . . . and ran" (v. 8).

The First Eyewitnesses—Seeing and Hearing
Matthew 28:1–8

The first message of the resurrection is essentially, "Go tell" (vv. 6–7). The eyewitnesses were the well-known women who had followed Jesus. Mary Magdalene, from the village of Magdala on the western side of the Sea of Galilee, was present at the cross (Matt. 27:56–57) and had ministered to the Lord during His ministry (Luke 8:2–3). She played a prominent role in all four Gospels during the resurrection (Mark 16; Luke 24:9–10; John 20:1) and is the first evangelist, along with "the other Mary" (the mother of the apostle "James the Less" (Mark.15:40), to tell the story of the empty tomb. They had gone to the tomb for the purpose of anointing the body of Jesus with spices for burial (Mark 16:1). They could not have expected to find an angel and the resurrected Christ. The women had come to offer a final ministry to the dead body of Jesus. Instead, they became part of God's plan of salvation through the ever-living Son of God! In both Roman law and Jewish culture, women could not offer evidence or testimony in court. Therefore, the fact that the women were given the privilege of being the first to tell the story of the empty tomb speaks to the historical accuracy of the event since no one would have invented that detail.

While the New Testament nowhere describes how the resurrection occurred, the insistence of the angel at the tomb is that it had, in fact, occurred. The angel offered no explanation of the miracle; instead he focused on the eyewitnesses' responsibility to tell what they had seen, namely an empty tomb (v. 7). The women are an example of evangelistic witness for every generation. They went about their work quickly, with joy, and with a deliberate target audience (v. 8).

Jesus Is Alive
Matthew 28:9–10

After introducing the reader to the supporting cast of the resurrection drama, Matthew turns his attention to Jesus who is fully alive and ready to reinforce the main message of the resurrection. Jesus appeared to guarantee that what the women saw at the empty tomb was, in fact, true; and He, Himself, insists on their mission: "Go and tell" (v. 10, NIV).

The False Report
Matthew 28:11–15

Once the guards came to their senses, they had a problem. They had been given the responsibility of guarding the tomb, and their failure was conspicuous. Pilate had been clear in his instructions; "Make the tomb as secure as you know how" (Matt. 27:65, NIV). That security included the seal of Rome (Matt. 27:66) and thus carried the death penalty for failure to protect it or for maliciously breaking it. The seal might have been a cord stretched across the stone and marked or "sealed" with the emblem of the empire (see Dan. 6:17). The Jewish leaders recognized the dilemma of the resurrection and attempted immediately to discredit the event by bribing the guards (who were probably more than happy to comply with any story that might keep them alive) and spreading a rumor that was still commonly retold by the time Matthew wrote his Gospel (v. 15). The improbability of someone rolling the stone away from the tomb and escaping with the body of Jesus without waking the guards is obvious. The stone was too big for even three women to move (Mark 16:3) and would have, therefore, been tediously heavy, requiring multiple laborers, noisily grinding stone against stone in the late-night silence of the garden. It was an impossible task to get away with and therefore resists any credibility as an explanation. One thing was certain, however: the body was gone. As in every generation, Jesus' enemies worked against the truth to attempt, by any means at hand, to silence the message of the evangelists.

The Great Commission
Matthew 28:16–20

Jesus had entrusted the women with the responsibility of arranging a meeting with the apostles in the northern region of Galilee (v. 10). They would see Jesus for themselves later that day (Luke 24:36), but the women were to deliver the message that all of the disciples must meet Jesus back home in the hill country near the Sea of Galilee where it all began.

It is unclear exactly how long after the resurrection the meeting with Jesus and His apostles took place. Jerusalem, where the crucifixion and resurrection took place, is about one hundred miles from the Sea of Galilee, and it would have taken the disciples a few days to walk home to meet the Lord. Neither is it clear exactly where the "mountain" was located where Jesus had arranged to meet the disciples (v. 16), except that it was in Galilee, an area surrounded by numerous hills and mountains. What is clear is that Jesus was giving His followers a worldwide vision and evangelistic mission. Their years of training under Jesus' tutelage were coming to an end, but their work was just beginning.

For a section of Scripture so well known as the Great Commission, so analyzed and so important to the mission of the church, it is surprisingly brief. There is an almost shocking economy of words. After all, these words have launched mission movements that have reached into cultures around the world. These few words, fewer than ninety in the Greek New Testament, have defined the direction of the church for two thousand years. What did Jesus say so succinctly that has inspired so much activity for so long?

The reaction of the disciples to seeing Jesus on the mountain was mixed. Some worshipped while others doubted (v. 17). The word *doubt* in the original language comes from the words *two* and *stand* and suggests someone standing in two ways. We might say the person is vacillating, shifting from one foot to the other. Whoever the doubters were, the suggestion is that they were hesitant and uncertain. Nevertheless, Jesus addressed the doubters and worshippers alike with the same instructions insisting they evangelize the world.

The disciples probably did not understand fully what Jesus was saying to them, as evidenced by their preoccupations at a later date. When they met Jesus back in Jerusalem sometime later, they were still focused on the nationalism of a restored Israel (Acts 1:6). Taking the opportunity of their shortsighted misunderstanding, Jesus reiterated the message of the Great Commission (Acts 1:8; Matt. 28:16–20). Given the disciples' uncertainty about the scope of their new mission, Jesus must have anticipated their uneasiness about their ability or even safety of going forward with a message that had resulted in the Lord's violent death and the disciples' fears about persecution that followed (John 20:19). Jesus assured them of His authority, which was like that of God Himself. Jesus claimed not a regional authority, but instead He had received "all authority . . . in heaven and on earth" (Matt. 28:18). The word *authority* is the Greek word meaning the "right." We should go everywhere with the gospel, therefore, because Jesus has the authority to send us anywhere at any time.

Next Jesus unveiled the specifics of His plan. The church is to "make disciples" (v. 19). In other words, what Jesus had done for each of them, they were now to do for others. The phrase "make disciples" is an imperative, and thus, grammatically, it is the strongest verb in the sentence. The word *disciple* in the Greek New Testament literally means a pupil or a learner, one whose mind has been directed. The emphasis however is not merely on the acquisition of more information. Instead, it is the knowledge learned from the repeated practice of an action. A disciple is one who is practiced in the disciplines of a way of life. Jesus commanded the church to make disciples everywhere. The implied promise is that there would be disciples "of all the nations" (v. 19). Israel's borders had evaporated in favor of a worldwide mission.

Jesus left no doubt about the end result of discipleship. The words "baptizing" (v. 19) and "teaching" (v. 20) are both participles and thus act as a "verbal noun" in support of the main verb. In other words, making disciples is what the church does, and baptizing them and teaching them is how we do it (vv. 19–20).

The practice of baptism was common in the New Testament (Matt. 3:6, 11, 13–16; Mark 1:4; Luke 3:7; John 4:1; Acts 2:41). The word means "to immerse" and was originally practiced by Jews as a self-immersion prior to entering the temple or for other times of ritual cleansing. The impressive baptismal pools used by the Jews, called mikvahs, are still clearly visible in Jerusalem outside the Temple Mount and at Qumran where the Dead Sea Scrolls were discovered. John the Baptist popularized the practice as a spiritual response to his call for repentance, and the ministry of Jesus involved baptism as a sign of discipleship (John 4:1). When Jesus instructed His followers to baptize new believers, they understood that they were to carry on the work He Himself had begun.

Teaching is likewise an extension of the ministry of Jesus, who was often called "Rabbi" or "Teacher" (Mark 9:5; John 20:16; etc.) The emphasis in the Great Commission, however, is not on the teacher but the teaching. The church is to instruct new believers to "obey" everything Jesus had taught (v. 20, NIV).

Having described the mission of the church in simple and familiar terms, Jesus gave them one final encouragement. He promised to be with us always. The Gospel began with the promise of the God who would be "with us" (Matt. 1:22–23). It concludes with the promise of the Son of God who will be with us always as we evangelize the world (Matt. 28:20).

For Memory and Meditation

"Go therefore and make disciples of all the nations, baptizing them in the name of the Father and the Son and the Holy Spirit, teaching them to observe all that I commanded you; and lo, I am with you always, even to the end of the age." Matthew 28:19–20

Pentecost and the Birth
of the Church, Part 1

Focal Text: Acts 1–2

How did a small group of nonmilitary men and women with
virtually no political clout, impoverished financial resources,
and all the common travel and communication limitations
of the first century change the world in their lifetimes? What
was their secret? Clearly they had help, and that help was the
power of the Holy Spirit!

The New Testament book of Acts could be known as the
"Acts of the Holy Spirit." For instance, Luke (author of the books
Luke and Acts) mentions the "Holy Spirit" more than Matthew,
Mark, and John combined. In the book of Acts, the number of
occurrences of the phrase "Holy Spirit" triples.

Luke was fascinated by the Holy Spirit, especially as He
empowered the early church for witness. The miracles of healing and other supernatural demonstrations, which we natu-
rally associate with the Holy Spirit, are surprisingly not where
Luke usually emphasizes the power of the Holy Spirit (Acts
3:6; 16:18; 19:13). Instead, Luke emphasizes the essential role
played by the Holy Spirit in empowering the apostles and others to evangelize the world (Acts 1:8; 4:8–10; 4:31; 8:28–29, 39).

Promise
Acts 1:4–5

After His resurrection Jesus appeared to His followers to reassure and instruct them over a period of forty days (Acts 1:3). It is easy to imagine their sense of expectancy about what might happen next. They were, however, focused on the wrong objectives. They had a shortsighted, nationalistic expectation (1:6), and Jesus knew they were not ready to represent Him.

Luke concluded his Gospel and opened Acts with similar themes (Luke 24:45–49; Acts 1:4–8) concerning the apostles' need for preparation prior to witnessing. Both times Jesus emphasized a time of waiting for the gift of the Holy Spirit's presence (Luke 24:49; Acts 1:4).

Jesus was emphatic about the need to stop before they could go. They were to stay in Jerusalem (even though they were all from Galilee), and they were to "stay" or "wait" (Luke 24:49; Acts 1:4). The word translated "wait" in Acts 1:4 occurs nowhere else in the Greek New Testament. It is made up of two common words and literally means "to remain around" or "to dwell near." In our vernacular we might even say, "Hang around." The parallel word translated "stay" in Luke 24:49 literally means "sit down" or "stop moving." At a time when the apostles had a life-changing message, to our surprise Jesus essentially said, "Don't move a muscle!" They needed the promised Holy Spirit in order to be effective.

Jesus called the experience of receiving the Holy Spirit being "baptized with the Holy Spirit" (v. 5). The terminology "baptism in the Spirit" creates debate today because it is used by Christians in different ways. It is beyond the scope of this study to explore the ways Christians have interpreted the term "baptized with the Holy Spirit" so we will focus on the text itself.

The promise of a baptism with the Holy Spirit was not original to Jesus because it was part of the predictions of John the Baptist a few years earlier. He had promised that Jesus would "baptize you with the Holy Spirit" (Matt. 3:11; Mark 1:8; John 1:33). The word translated "baptism" was the same one used to describe the immersions John practiced in the Jordan River (John 1:28). The baptism with the Holy Spirit, therefore, would be an immersion in or with the Spirit comparable to being submerged in water.

Finally, the term "baptized with the Holy Spirit" (Acts 1:5) is not used again in the book of Acts. Instead, the work of the Holy Spirit is described as a "filling with the Holy Spirit" (Acts 2:4; 4:31; 6:5; 9:17), "receiving the Spirit" (8:15–17; 10:47), the Spirit "coming on" them (10:44), and being "poured out" on them (10:45). All of these terms appear to be mostly interchangeable.

What does all of this suggest about our need today as the people of God? Does the church of Jesus need the Holy Spirit any less in the twenty-first century? Regardless of what we call this experience of spiritual endowment, the fullness of the Holy Spirit was essential to the plan of God then, and it must be an essential for us today. We need the Holy Spirit!

Power
Acts 1:6–8

The disciples were anxious for news about the political future of Israel (v. 6). Perhaps they were imagining a place of prominence in what they could only perceive as an earthly kingdom for Jesus headquartered in Jerusalem (Mark 10:37). Jesus, however, had a much bigger vision for His people than simply holding positions in a politically restructured Israel. Instead, He promised them power from heaven (v. 8).

The word *power* in the Greek is like the English word *dynamic*. It is the word which means "the ability" to perform or "the strength" to act in capable and powerful ways. Even if the apostles' impatience for the restoration of "the kingdom to Israel" (v. 6) is understandable, it was unacceptable to Jesus. He wanted them to reach the world beginning at Jerusalem and extending out to "the remotest part of the earth" (v. 8). Only a baptism of God's Holy Spirit could prepare them for that mission.

Without the Spirit they could not imagine the worldwide mission, and they apparently had no taste for it. Once they experienced the power of the Holy Spirit, however, Jesus assured them that they would in fact be His "witnesses," a word that means they would tell the world what Jesus had done. The word *witness* (v. 8) is the Greek word *martus* from which we get the English word *martyr*. While in Jesus' time it described a witness in a legal trial, in much the same way we use the word today, in time it came to mean "one who is willing to die for what he believes." It developed that meaning because so many people, because of their witness for Christ, were willing to lay down their lives in order to preach the Word. Jesus promised the Holy Spirit so the church could witness.

Prayer
Acts 1:12–14

Armin Gesswein once insightfully observed, "The early church didn't attend a prayer meeting. The early church was a prayer meeting!"[1] It is impossible to deny the role prayer played in the early church, and no New Testament author recognized that more than Luke. In fact, Luke's Gospel mentions prayer almost twice as often as any of the other three; and his second volume, Acts, is similarly full of references and examples of prayer. Appropriately, the apostles and the other disciples with them (v. 13) interpreted the instructions of Jesus to "wait" (v. 5) as an occasion to pray in anticipation of Jesus' promise of the coming of the Holy Spirit.

The prayer meeting took place mostly in an upstairs room just inside the city walls of Jerusalem (v. 12), where they devoted themselves to congregational prayer. The words translated "joined together" (v. 14, NIV) in Greek are in the imperfect tense suggesting continuous or repeated action. They never stopped praying! The word *devoting* (v. 14) literally means "one passion," a word which emphasizes the fact that the group shared a common and mutual zeal in prayer. Luke specifies that all of the disciples, which included the apostles, the women along with Mary the mother of Jesus (mentioned here in the New Testament for the last time), the brothers of Jesus, and an unnamed group were part of the prayers (vv. 13–15) which continued for ten days. Luke adds the additional detail that when the group was not in the "upper room" devoting themselves to prayer, they could be found "continually in the temple praising God" (Luke 24:53). The congregational aspect of prayer demonstrated among the disciples prior to Pentecost is the first of multiple examples throughout the rest of Acts. While prayer will occur numerous times throughout the book, in almost every example it will be with a group rather than an individual.

The power of congregational prayer is one of the subtle reminders throughout the book of Acts that the Lord has equipped the church with everything needed to fulfill the staggeringly immense task of taking the gospel to the world. What the church prays about in the book of Acts in nearly every occasion, it accomplishes by the power of the Holy Spirit of God. The early church discovered that prayer moves the Hand that moves the world.

Pentecost
Acts 2:1–15

Pentecost (which means "fiftieth") is called "the Feast of Weeks" in the Old Testament (Lev. 23:15–21) and was one of the three most important annual religious festivals in Jewish life, occurring exactly fifty days after Passover. While secondary in importance to Passover, it would have been better attended since it occurred in early summer when roads were dry and the weather was more agreeable.

For the followers of Jesus, the day of prayer began like all the others. They were strategically united, as is obvious from the observation that "they were all together in one place" (v. 1). That phrase may appear to be redundant because if they were in "one place" they were obviously together. Yet when considered more closely, most of us can agree that people can share the same address and not be truly "together." The disciples, however, were "together" (the same word used in Acts 1 meaning "one passion"). They all shared the same zeal.

At just before 9:00 a.m. (v. 15) the Holy Spirit interrupted their prayer with the sound of blowing wind and a visible fire from heaven (vv. 2–3). They had been praying for almost two weeks, but when the answer came, they were caught off guard when events began "suddenly." The first thing they noticed was a sound (the Greek word is *echos*) equivalent to a hurricane described as "a violent rushing wind." The mighty wind was rushing "from heaven." It is not apparent that the wind was actually blowing. The emphasis is on the sound like a violent wind rather than on the physical wind itself. What is of interest is this: the words *wind* and *spirit* come from the same Greek root word. What was happening to them had been promised: the Holy Spirit was coming.

The next thing they noticed is unprecedented in Scripture. Luke says, "There appeared to them tongues as of fire distributing themselves, and they rested on each one of them" (v. 3). They actually saw (the word is *optonomai* in Greek) the tongues of fire. Then the mysterious tongues of fire separated, as if spreading out on command. At that point every disciple was equally anointed with the tongues of fire. Could any symbol be more dramatic or more fitting for a group charged with the responsibility of carrying a message than that of receiving tongues set aflame?

At that point, having all been filled with the Holy Spirit (v. 4), the disciples began preaching in the multiple languages represented at the festival of Pentecost. Although the meaning of *tongues* is still debated today, the miracle of Pentecost was clearly not an unknown prayer language but instead a gift of known languages for missionary, cross-cultural evangelism (see vv. 5–12). The Spirit had supernaturally enabled them to speak languages they had never learned.

The lessons of Pentecost extend to our present time. Worldwide evangelism has never been more urgent than it is today. The church is still charged by the Lord with being a "witness," and we are still as helpless as ever without the Holy Spirit.

If the early church found great success through waiting on God in prayer for the announcing of the Spirit, why would we not do the same? Every revival in history has been preceded by prayer, and our time will be no exception. If we are to be His witnesses, we need to seek God's face in prayer and personally experience the power of the Holy Spirit. Nothing else will do.

Next week we will explore how the miracle of Pentecost birthed the church and ignited a worldwide evangelistic movement that continues today.

For Memory and Meditation

"You will receive power when the Holy Spirit has come upon you; and you shall be My witnesses both in Jerusalem, and in all Judea and Samaria, and even to the remotest part of the earth." Acts 1:8

---

[1] Armin Gesswein, *With One Accord in One Place* (Camp Hill, PA: Christian Publications, 1978), 13.

Pentecost and the Birth of the Church, Part 2

Focal Text: Acts 2:13–47

A drive through any American city provides a good example of the variety of churches today. Churches differ in worship style, governance, and doctrinal emphasis. Yet regardless of these differences, Scripture describes a day when it all began as one church! That first church was a powerful portrait of what God can do in a redeemed people. What about their experiences then, at the birth of the church, might be a blueprint for our churches now?

The First Sermon of the Church
Acts 2:14–36

There were about 120 disciples in the prayer meetings (Acts 1:15), and all of them "began to speak with other tongues" (Acts 2:4). The crowds clearly heard that (vv. 7–8), but Peter's sermon is represented in the text. The entire group of apostles must have witnessed throughout the crowd, but Peter's message was the focal point (v. 14).

Luke, the author of Acts, used the sermons and speeches of the early church to help tell his story. In fact, approximately one-third of the verses, about three hundred of about a thousand comprising the entire book are speeches by Peter, Paul, and a few others. In the early chapters of Acts, Peter is the visible leader of the church and the most obvious figure of its rapid growth. The first sermon of the church, not surprisingly therefore, showcases Peter's role as the spokesman of the movement (vv. 14–36).

If the portrayal of the early church at Pentecost is a blueprint for the church today, perhaps elements of that first sermon are blueprints for preaching too. The striking thing about the sermon is its heavy reliance on Scripture. Peter had followed Jesus in the flesh, had seen the empty tomb, and had fellowship with the resurrected Lord. If anyone had a personal testimony full of relevant narrative, it was Peter, but surprisingly he said nothing at all about his personal association with Jesus of Nazareth. Instead, of the twenty-three verses that recount Peter's sermon, twelve of those verses, half, are direct quotations from the Old Testament (vv. 16–21, 25–28, 31, 34–35).

What was the theme of the sermon? First Peter had to explain the coming of the Spirit and how that event fit into God's prophetic plan. He found his authority in Joel's prophecy concerning "the last days" which would be full of signs, miracles, and the salvation of "everyone who calls on the name of the LORD" brought about by an outpouring of the Spirit (vv. 17–21; Joel 2:28–32). From there Peter turned his attention to Jesus as the Savior, brutally nailed to the cross and raised from the dead by the power of God (vv. 22–24). The resurrection dominates the sermon with an explanation based on a descriptive psalm of David, which speaks of the Holy One of God not seeing decay after death (vv. 25–35).

As the sermon drew to a conclusion, Peter made one of the most dramatic statements found in the New Testament (v. 36). It was unapologetically direct as the apostle indicted "all . . . Israel" for the crucifixion of Jesus that had occurred in Jerusalem only fifty days earlier. The sermon presents a clear comparison between man and God's perception of Jesus and His work. Peter reminded his hearers that the one "you crucified" God has made "both Lord and Christ" (v. 36).

The titles "Lord" and "Christ" applied to Jesus in Peter's incisive declaration are loaded with theological implications (v. 36). The use of these two provocative terms makes clear that from the earliest days of the church's proclamations about Jesus, He is more than any of His contemporaries had comprehended. Furthermore, far from being assigned equality with God at some later church council, Jesus was Lord and Christ from the infancy of the church's understanding of Him.

The word *Lord* comes from a Greek word meaning "to have power and authority or supreme rank." It is sometimes used in the New Testament as a form of respect for a man, not unlike the English word *sir* (John 4:15, 19). Usually however, we are to understand the term to refer to God. For example, before and after the birth of Jesus, "the angel of the Lord" appeared to Joseph (Matt. 1:20, 24; 2:19; etc.). In another example, when Jesus confronted Satan, He reminded the devil not to "put the Lord your God to the test," and that we should "worship the Lord your God, and serve Him only" (Matt. 4:7–10). The examples in the New Testament of the word *Lord* as applied to God are abundant. The declaration of Peter, therefore, concerning the lordship of Jesus, makes clear that Jesus is coequal with the Father and reigns as Lord.

Equally significant is the term *Christ*. It occurs hundreds of times in the New Testament and is the Greek equivalent of the Hebrew word *Messiah*. Both words mean "the anointed one." The first verse of the New Testament identifies Jesus as the "Messiah" (Matt. 1:1), and He has been identified as the Christ ever since. The development of the concept of a coming ruler known as the "Messiah" is predicted most clearly in the book of Daniel, when he prophesied, "the Anointed One [Messiah], the ruler comes" (Dan. 9:25, NIV), and later, "the Messiah will be cut off and will have nothing" (Dan. 9:26). Daniel's prophecy of the "Anointed One," therefore, is the clearest Old Testament reference to a coming ruler who would be the "Messiah."

During the years between the close of the Old Testament and the birth of Jesus, the Jewish people had become accustomed to rabbinical teaching about the Messiah. King Herod, for instance, inquired of the priests and teachers as to "where the Messiah was to be born" (Matt. 2:4). That inquiry was spurred by wise men asking where the "King of the Jews" would be born (Matt. 2:2). Even Herod associated the "King of the Jews" with the "Messiah," and the scribal team wasted no time giving the king the correct answer. They said Messiah would be born in Bethlehem even though the word *Messiah* does not occur in Micah's prophecy. Instead, "a ruler who will shepherd My people Israel" is promised (Matt. 2:6; Mic. 5:2). Yet the *ruler*, the *shepherd*, and the *king of the Jews* were all synonymous with *Messiah* by the time of Jesus' birth.

The messianic expectations of the Jews were also clear when John the Baptist arrived on the scene. The Jewish leaders, trying to identify him with some prophetic figure from Scripture, asked him who he was. His first denial was probably in response to a direct question from the Jews about the Messiah because John answered, "I am not the Christ" (John 1:19–20). The term *Christ* or *Messiah* was common by the time of Jesus and resulted from multiple biblical prophecies pointing to a ruler sent from God who would bless the people and usher in the last days. Therefore, when Peter said Jesus was "the Christ" (Acts 2:36), he was identifying Him as the One predicted in Scripture and expected by the Jewish people.

The Response to the Sermon
Acts 2:37–41

The first sermon of the church called for and received an immediate response (v. 37). The people were "pierced to the heart," a phrase which indicates they were made painfully aware of their personal sin and role in the crucifixion. The word *heart* comes from the Greek word *kardia*, from which we get the English word *cardiac*. In other words, they felt the sharp sting of the sermon to the depths of their being. As a result they asked what they should do about the sense of conviction that had swept over them.

Peter's instructions were direct. He advised them to "repent, and . . . be baptized" (v. 38). The word *repent* literally means "to change your mind." Their view of Jesus had been incorrect and in direct opposition to the will of God (v. 36). Repentance calls for action, and baptism was the visible sign of agreeing with God about sin.

Like John the Baptist and Jesus before them (John 4:1), the apostles would henceforth insist on baptism as the sign of true repentance. The English text that reads, "be baptized . . . for the forgiveness of your sins" (v. 38) can be accurately translated "be baptized . . . as a result of the remission of sins" and does not teach baptism as a means of salvation. Instead, baptism is the public evidence of repentance, which begins invisibly in the heart.

As a result of the convicting power of that first sermon, the prayer meeting of the upper room surged to more than three thousand followers of Jesus. The church was born in a prayer meeting and immediately grew from an evangelistic sermon. The connection between congregational prayer, the anointing of the Holy Spirit, and confrontational, evangelistic preaching is still an effective combination for the twenty-first-century church.

The Community of Jesus
Acts 2:42–47

In the Great Commission, Jesus had instructed the apostles to do three specific things. He said they should make disciples, baptize them, and teach them all that He had commanded (Matt. 28:19–20). As soon as the apostles had an opportunity to obey the Lord, they made disciples (Acts 2:40–41), they baptized them (v. 41), and they taught them (v. 42). If the twenty-first-century church follows the Lord's direction as closely as the early church did in making, baptizing, and teaching disciples, it will continue to build on a strong foundation.

One of Luke's literary devices is the use of summaries. It is as if he pauses the action to focus the reader's attention on a desirable moment in the life in the early church. Such a summary (vv. 42–47) is found in "a beautiful little cameo of the Spirit–filled church.[1] The apostles began immediately teaching the new believers (v. 42). From its earliest days the church was a school for discipleship based on the study of Scripture rather than spiritual experience alone. The word *devoted* (v. 42) describes perseverance in learning rather than a "crash course." The "apostles' teaching" has been preserved for us as the New Testament so that what they learned in the early church, we are still learning today!

The church was also a place where the various countries and language groups represented (Acts 2: 5–11) were uniquely blended into a loving family. They shared "fellowship" (v. 42) (the Greek word is used only here in the book of Acts), which literally means "community." The fellowship was an ongoing reality rather than a single event. It was a part of what they were "devoted" to do. In addition, the church was a community because they took their meals together (v. 42), showing the closeness of the large group, and probably implying that the church began partaking of the Lord's Supper or Communion together. Luke alone of the Gospel writers recalled Jesus' instruction to "remember me" when taking the Lord's Supper (Luke 22:19) and no doubt saw the fellowship meal of the early church as a fulfillment of the Lord's request.

The early church was also a praying church (v. 42). The church was born in the upper room while the disciples were praying (Acts 1:14; 2:1), and Luke makes clear that the prayer meeting continued in the infant church. The apostolic ministry of miracles clearly added God's stamp of approval on the church (vv. 19, 43; Joel 2:30) and as a result, filled everyone involved with a reverential "awe" (v. 43). The community of Jesus also demonstrated the seriousness and dedication of their new faith by selling personal property and sharing the proceeds with the entire church (v. 45). They were a happy group who endeared themselves to the city as they praised God and shared their lives together (vv. 46–47). And as they were teaching, sharing, and praying, "the Lord was adding to their number day by day those who were being saved" (v. 47).

No wonder Luke gives us this summary. A Bible–believing, loving, praying, miraculous, Spirit–filled, evangelistic community of faith will always be the blueprint for the church.

For Memory and Meditation

"They were continually devoting themselves to the apostles' teaching and to fellowship, to the breaking of bread and to prayer." Acts 2:42

---

[1] John R. W. Stott, *The Bible Speaks Today: The Message of Acts* (Downers Grove, IL: Inter–Varsity Press, 1990), 81.

The Conversion of the Apostle Paul

Focal Text: Acts 9

Major American cities and world-famous churches and cathedrals bear his name. The apostle Paul is, by most accounts, the most influential follower of Jesus Christ who has ever lived. He wrote nearly half of the New Testament and led the way in evangelizing the Gentile world of the Roman Empire. His conversion to Christ is one of the most significant events in human history and undoubtedly changed the course of Western civilization. Most Christians probably feel they know Paul. Yet while his thoughts have been read and examined for two thousand years, we know little about the man himself except for a few fragments of his story pieced together from the New Testament.

Who Is Paul?

He was born in Tarsus, the capital city of Cilicia, in the south central part of modern Turkey, near the Mediterranean Sea coast (Acts 22:3). In 66 BC the inhabitants of Tarsus became Roman citizens, and Paul would make good use of his natural-born citizenship when it served his interests (Acts 16:37–39; 22:23–29; 25:10–12). Tarsus was known for felt made from the wool of black goats and craft guilds like garment makers, tent making, and leather workers. Paul probably learned the trade of tent making in his hometown where, according to Jewish tradition, his family was in the tent-making guild (Acts 18:3).

Paul, or Saul, of Tarsus as he was originally known, spent a large part of his young life in Jerusalem where he was formally educated under the rabbinical tutelage of the famous Jewish scholar Gamaliel (Acts 22:3). Gamaliel was perhaps the most influential Pharisee in Israel and a respected voice in the Sanhedrin. He actually tried to discourage the open hostility toward Christianity by arguing that God would judge the merits of the Christian claims as to whether they were true or false (Acts 5:34–39).

Paul had earlier followed his teacher's sectarian lead and joined himself to the religious group known as the Pharisees (Phil. 3:5). The Pharisees were meticulous about keeping the laws of the Old Testament and were the leaders of the local synagogues where they influenced the daily religious lives of the average people of Israel. In their role as leaders in the religious community, with a highly developed sense of legalistic religious views, they became frequent critics of Jesus during His brief public ministry (Matt. 12:2; Mark 12:13; Luke 19:39; etc.). Paul excelled as a Pharisee (Phil. 3:6) and was a rising star among the small but influential sect (Gal. 1:14).

His ravenous insistence that other Jews conform to his particular viewpoint led to a murderous rampage against the infant church while he was still a young man. He had been an eyewitness and passive accomplice to the public and ruthless assassination of the Christian deacon Stephen (Acts 7:58; 8:1). That brutal event, led by a religious mob with a taste for blood, excited the passions of young Saul of Tarsus who was probably in his late twenties at the time. From that point he went on a kind of killing spree, admitting later, "I persecuted this Way to the death, binding and putting both men and women into prison" (Acts 22:4). During this self-appointed mission of vengeance, Saul came face-to-face with the Head of the movement he had tried so hard to destroy.

The Damascus Road
Acts 9:1–9

The conversion of Saul of Tarsus may be the most famous in history. The colloquial phrase "a Damascus road experience," even used outside religious circles, is a common way to describe a sudden change of opinion and originated from Paul's conversion. Luke recognized the significance of Paul's conversion and recorded certain details of the conversion three times in the book of Acts (9:1-9; 22:3–21; 26:2–23).

The story of Saul of Tarsus began at the stoning of Stephen (7:58–60; 8:1) and resumes with the hostile picture of Saul emboldened by the deacon's murder, "breathing threats and murder," a phrase which literally describes Saul's willingness to hound the young church's members to their death as if he were a wild animal chasing down its prey (Acts 9:1).

Probably following the persecution of the church that erupted after Stephen's death, a group of Jewish Christians settled in Damascus, Syria (the oldest city in the world today), approximately 135 miles north and slightly east of Jerusalem. Damascus was an important commercial center in the first century and a good place for Christians to work and live. Those believers became the target of Saul who acquired "letters" from the high priest, something akin to modern extradition papers, permitting him to arrest the Jewish Christians, bring them back to Jerusalem, and hopefully watch them die as Stephen had died. His quest was interrupted, however, by a blinding light which appeared so suddenly and dramatically on the outskirts of Damascus that it knocked the aggressive bounty hunter to the ground (vv. 3–4).

The story of Saul's angry authority was dramatically reversed when the Lord Jesus appeared and demanded an accounting for Saul's outrageous actions. Saul was arrogant and unstoppable until the flash of light from Jesus knocked the bravado out of him. The word translated "flashed," describing the heavenly light (v. 3), comes from the Greek root word *aster* from which we get the English word *star*. This impressive blast of heaven's light temporarily blinded Saul (v. 8–9). The first recorded words of Paul in the New Testament are, "Who are You, Lord?" The rest of his life would be enthusiastically devoted to answering that question (v. 5).

Once Jesus appeared, the focus obviously shifted to Him. His authoritative words and brilliant glory clearly trumped the "letters" from the high priest, and Saul unhesitatingly obeyed the Lord's instructions to enter the city under the authority of Christ, rather than as His enemy (vv. 6–8). The drama could not be more obvious. The chapter begins with Saul on his way to Damascus eager to exercise his newfound power and authority, but he enters the city blind and led by the hand, humbled by the One he had sworn to defeat (vv. 7–9).

The Discipling of Paul
Acts 9:10–19

Saul had excelled as a Jewish Pharisee, but he had to start from the beginning as a Christian disciple. When he met Jesus on the road, he discovered lordship. Now it was time to learn about discipleship and fellowship. The process of spiritual growth had begun before Ananias got involved. Once in Damascus, Saul fasted and prayed for three days (vv. 9, 11). These two disciplines were common to Saul the Jewish Pharisee, but no doubt they took on an entirely new significance after he met Jesus.

While Scripture does not tell us what Paul was praying about, the context allows us to consider the strong probability that Saul was deeply repentant as he considered for three days how wrong he had been. He must have considered the impact his hatred had on the innocent lives of others, including the deacon Stephen who died with "the face of an angel" (Acts 6:15), "full of the Holy Spirit" (7:55), confessing that he could see "the Son of Man standing at the right hand of God" (7:56), and praying that God would forgive Saul and the others for stoning him to death (7:60). How could that scene not have replayed through Saul's mind repeatedly and dominated the theme of his prayers now that he had seen the ascended Lord for himself? Regardless of the now unknowable content of Paul's initial prayers, the fact of his private three-day prayer meeting was the first step in the discipling process of the man who would later encourage all of us to "pray without ceasing" (1 Thess. 5:17).

The man called to introduce Saul to further steps in the process of Christian maturity was Ananias, about whom little is known apart from what can be gleaned from this passage and one other. Years after Paul's conversion, while sharing his testimony, he described Ananias as a leading Jewish Christian who had gained the respect of the Jews in Damascus because of his devotion to the law of Moses (Acts 22:12). He seems then to have been the perfect candidate to lead Paul through the new believer's class of life. He was a Jew with a thorough knowledge of the Old Testament but one who himself had become a follower of Christ.

Ananias was surprised by the vision from the Lord because Saul's rage against the church had become widely known (Acts 9:13). Once convinced of God's plan (vv. 15–16), Ananias went to Straight Street (still a busy road in modern Damascus) where he found Saul. He wasted no time embracing Saul as a "brother" (v. 17) helping him feel the warmth of the Christian family, the same family Saul had previously been only too happy to drag to their deaths. This is one of the foundations of the growing Christian life: embracing the notion of fellowship in the body of Christ.

In addition, Saul was to learn his first lesson about the indwelling power of the Holy Spirit (v. 17). Ananias used the term "filled with the Holy Spirit." The word *filled* is from the same root as Paul's own use of the word years later when he instructed all believers to be "filled with the Holy Spirit" (Eph. 5:18). Rather than a reward for growth, the fullness of the Holy Spirit is a force God uses to bring about growth in a new believer. Unlike the experience at Pentecost, there are no recorded dramatic signs of the Holy Spirit's presence with Saul. Like the Pentecost experience, however, the dynamic power of God, evident in his later ministry, was abundant proof of the Spirit's fullness in his life.

After Ananias laid his hands on Saul so Saul could miraculously regain his sight (v.18), the next step in the discipleship of the new believer was to baptize him. Baptism was the most visible way for a believer to express his identification with Christ and His church (v. 18). Baptism had been commanded for all disciples by the resurrected Lord (Matt. 28:19) and was the pattern of discipleship in the book of Acts (2:41; 8:38; 10:48; etc.).

The Early Ministry of Paul
Acts 9:20–25

The Lord had instructed Ananias that Saul was to be His "chosen instrument" to three specific groups: "the Gentiles and kings and the sons of Israel" (v. 15). Saul wasted no time working to fulfill his calling. For the next three years Paul stayed in Damascus, studying and preaching (Gal. 1:17–18). During those years Paul grew personally through his interaction with the Christian community in Damascus, the same group he had originally come to destroy. With them he learned to apply the Scripture to the events and teachings from Christ's life and ministry (Acts 9:19). Armed with his background as an Old Testament scholar, trained under the best rabbi in Israel, his newfound faith in the living Christ, the power of the indwelling Holy Spirit, and the instruction from other disciples, such as Ananias and the believers in Damascus, Paul was eager to get to work.

The synagogues were the local assemblies of Jews in their neighborhoods. The synagogue system had been created during the Babylonian captivity of Judah as a way for Jews to gather for worship, Bible study, and prayer. Paul went to the synagogues "immediately" to "proclaim" that Jesus "is the Son of God" (Acts 9:20). The immediate reaction of the Jews who heard him was the same as that of Ananias when the Lord called on him to minister to Paul in the first place. They were "amazed" (v. 21) because Paul's reputation as a persecutor was well known. He had letters to these synagogues from the high priest in Jerusalem to arrest Christians; yet by the time he arrived, he was a Christian himself (vv. 21–22).

Jealousy led to a murder plot against Paul in Damascus. He had originally come to Damascus to persecute Christians, but he would leave town as a persecuted Christian (vv. 23–25). It was time for Paul to go to Jerusalem.

Paul in Jerusalem
Acts 9:26–30

Paul returned to Jerusalem after a three-year absence as a kind of man without a country. The Jewish leaders he had once been a part of could no longer welcome him, and the disciples were skeptical about him due to his previous persecution of the church (v. 26). At that point in the narrative, Paul met important Christians who would become a part of his future: Barnabas, his missionary traveling companion (13:1ff), and the apostles Peter and James (Gal. 1:18–20), who helped him find a welcome among the believers.

After this brief, two-week visit (Gal. 1:17–18), Paul fades from view in Luke's account, but the foundation has been laid. By the time Paul reemerges in Acts, he is a major player, and the rest of the book will center on his ministry for Christ and the worldwide expansion of the gospel.

For Memory and Meditation

"'Who are you, Lord?' Saul asked. 'I am Jesus, whom you are persecuting,' he replied. 'Now get up and go into the city, and you will be told what you must do.'" Acts 9:5–6

Church Growth

Focal Text: Acts 13–19

The church of Jesus Christ is the only organization in the world that exists for those who aren't yet its members. Reading the book of Acts convinces the reader that reaching the world is the plan and purpose of God. No nonviolent, nonmilitary, voluntary movement in history has ever grown so rapidly and effectively as the church of Jesus in the first century.

The spread of Christianity was, in fact, the extension of the miraculous and redemptive work of Jesus of Nazareth. Church growth throughout the Roman Empire was nothing less than the first "Jesus Movement." This chapter reviews some of the more well-known examples of that early church growth, especially in those cities that eventually became recipients of the books of the New Testament.

"A Light for the Gentiles"
Acts 13:1–48

The incredible surge of church growth throughout the Roman Empire began with an emphasis on gifted leadership, the power of prayer, and the Holy Spirit. Barnabas, introduced in Acts 4:36, had begun mentoring Paul for wider ministry (Acts 11:22–25). In one prayer service a small group of leaders, including Barnabas and Saul (as Paul was still known), met for an evangelistic strategy session (Acts 13:1). They were all engaged in continuous worship and fasting. In this spiritual "maternity ward" the Holy Spirit spoke to the group. He called out Barnabas and Saul to take an evangelistic mission trip (v. 2). It is not clear how the Spirit spoke, but the environment, prepared by intense prayer and fasting, invited the Spirit's specific direction. One can only imagine what could still be possible if we gathered with other disciples, desperate for a move of God, in an unhurried season of worship, prayer, and fasting to receive specific instructions for ministry in our own cities and through our own churches today!

The evangelistic, church-planting mission movement that began in the Spirit's presence would eventually stretch to the ends of the earth. Barnabas is the leader in these verses as he is always mentioned before Saul, his associate (Acts 11:22–26; 13:2). Soon their roles would be reversed, and the mission team would be known as Paul and Barnabas (v. 46). What God did next would leave the name of the apostle Paul woven inextricably into the fabric of church history.

Barnabas and Saul left what was known as Antioch of Syria (now in modern Turkey) and sailed to the isle of Cyprus where they started preaching (vv. 4–5). Cyprus was a likely first stop for several reasons: a witness had begun there a few years earlier (Acts 11:19–20), it was geographically nearby, and it was Barnabas's home (Acts 4:36). Barnabas might have had several important connections from which to draw as they traveled the relatively large island (13:6). On this first mission trip to Cyprus, Saul would become known as Paul (v. 9).

After a successful mission on Cyprus, the team eventually made their way to a second city called Antioch, this one distinguished by the name Pisidian Antioch. It was roughly three hundred miles northwest of the first city of Antioch, the town from which their journey had begun. Upon their arrival Paul and Barnabas found the Jewish synagogue, and Paul preached a sermon rich with Old Testament history, which appealed to his Jewish audience (vv. 16–22). Paul's message, however, was not intended as a Hebrew history lesson. Instead, he pressed the claims of Christ and the apostles, namely that Jesus was the fulfillment of Old Testament prophecy (vv. 26–41).

The next Sabbath Paul returned to speak, but this time he met resistance from the Jewish leaders who were jealous of the growing popularity of the mission team (vv. 44–45). At that point an important decision, one that had been some time in coming (Acts 9:15), was reached. Paul declared his intention to take the gospel to the Gentiles. Using Old Testament prophecy as his authority, the young missionary, growing more confident with each experience of ministry, changed the trajectory of Christianity forever, leading it out of the family of Jews into the wider audience of the entire world. As Paul saw it, he was being true not only to his calling as a Christian but also as a Jew since God had said through Isaiah, "I have placed You as a light for the Gentiles, that You may bring salvation to the ends of the earth" (Acts 13:47).

Church Growth in Philippi
Acts 16:11–36

About six years after the start of the first mission trip, Paul arrived in Philippi on the continent of Europe. On Paul's previous trip he had focused most of his time in what was then called Galatia in Asia Minor, what we know today as the mountains of northwestern and central Turkey. On this second trip, however, Paul focused on northern and southern Greece, or what was then called Macedonia. Paul's team made no distinction between Asia and Europe as it was all part of the Roman Empire. Today we recognize that Paul's westward expansion into Europe helped to set the stage for Christianity's dominate role in the history of Western civilization.

The first convert on European soil was Lydia, a Gentile businesswoman with a home in Philippi. Paul had been drawn by the Spirit into Macedonia through a dream he had in the city of Troas (Acts 16:8–10). Once in Philippi he arrived to what today is an impressive city of ruins, but Paul would have known it as the "leading city of the district of Macedonia" (v. 12). As was his strategic pattern in a new city, Paul hoped to begin his ministry in the local Jewish synagogue. However, in Philippi no synagogue existed, undoubtedly due to a small or virtually nonexistent Jewish population (v. 13). Where Paul had hoped to find a synagogue, he found a group of women at the shallow, narrow Gangites River, a few hundred yards outside of town (v. 13). The first person baptized on European soil was Lydia, an international business professional with a high-end client list that included priests and royalty, the only groups who ordinarily could afford her products (vv. 14–15). The first church in Europe probably started in her home.

After the conversion of Lydia and others associated with her, the second major conversion story in Philippi was a woman on the opposite end of the socioeconomic strata. While on their way to the prayer meeting one day, the missionaries met a young slave girl "who had a spirit by which she predicted the future" (v. 16, NIV). The Greek text makes clear that she was possessed by a demonic spirit. This was no harmless game. She was a victim of human trafficking and was only as good as the profits she brought to her owners (vv. 16, 19). When the "spirit" within her recognized Paul, she started involuntarily announc-ing the nature of his mission (vv. 17–18). This had gone on for days, and the distraction and absurdity finally became intolerable for Paul.

After Paul cast the demon out of the girl, her owners stirred up the city officials with false charges and had Paul arrested and sent to the city jail (vv. 19–23). The third major conversion occurs in prison. A miraculous earthquake allowed Paul and the other prisoners to escape, but they chose not to do so. Their demeanor and the accompanying verbal witness led the jailer to repent, receive Christ, and be baptized (vv. 25–34).

One lesson for church growth from the experiences in Philippi has to do with the inclusiveness of the New Testament church. The first church in Philippi was made up of a career woman, a slave with an occult past, and a working-class man with a family. Everyone is included in the good news about Jesus, and everybody needs His church.

Church Growth in Thessalonica
Acts 17:1–9

Today the biblical city of Thessalonica is the second largest city in Greece with a population of more than 300,000 people and a broader, urban population approaching one million residents called Thessaloniki. It was approximately one hundred miles from Philippi, and Paul's travel schedule indicates it was his intended destination, having passed through other cities to reach Thessalonica (v. 1). In the synagogue of Thessalonica, Paul found a receptive audience (vv. 2–4). He spent "three Sabbaths" explaining the Old Testament passages that point to Jesus as the fulfillment of messianic prophecy. The word *reasoned* (v. 2), used to describe Paul's teaching and preaching style, is the Greek word *dialegomai* from which we get the English word *dialogue* and suggests that Paul's work in the synagogues was more discussion than sermon.

Even though the initial work in Thessalonica was well received, eventually the Jewish leaders were "jealous," and following a riot, Paul left for another town about fifty miles away. The memories of his ministry in Thessalonica were good, however, because he would later write that the Thessalonian church was "an example to all the believers in Macedonia and in Achaia" (1 Thess. 1:7).

Church Growth in Corinth
Acts 18:1–11

After ministry in Berea and Athens (Acts 17:10–34), Paul went to the metropolitan city of Corinth. The area had been populated for thousands of years, but the city had been destroyed in the second century BC. Corinth was rebuilt by Julius Caesar in 44 BC and quickly grew to become the largest city in Greece by the time of Paul's visit.

Paul stayed in Corinth eighteen months (Acts 18:11), working as a tentmaker for a time with two other Jewish Christians (v. 3) while he preached and taught both Jews and Gentiles (vv. 5–7). Paul found success among the Greco-Roman Gentile population, forming a church by baptizing several of them (vv. 7–8). In Corinth the Lord Jesus appeared to Paul in a vision, reassuring him that He had "many people" in the city of Corinth, meaning there would be many more conversions and disciples (v. 9). Regardless of the growing opposition to the gospel (vv. 12–17), the Lord reminded Paul that he had nothing to fear because Jesus would be with him (v. 9). In ministry few rewards are more precious than the assurance to our hearts that God fights on our behalf and holds us close to Himself during the battle.

Church Growth in Ephesus
Acts 19:1–41

The city of Ephesus in modern Turkey lies in ruins today. In Paul's day, however, it was one of the most important cities in the Roman Empire. It was a seaport city with a twenty-five-thousand-seat Greek theater and a library, both still partially standing. It is easy to imagine why Paul flourished in the city of Ephesus.

Several ministries there stand out. A small sect of John the Baptist's disciples was active in Ephesus and experienced a kind of "Pentecost" after receiving Paul's message and the Holy Spirit (vv. 1–7). Paul performed "extraordinary miracles" at Ephesus (vv. 11–12), and a riot occurred as a direct result of his ministry (vv. 23–41). The riot reminds us that the gospel is not always received well, but we must keep preaching, teaching, and living it.

Another incident in Ephesus highlights the nature of our spiritual battle. In Ephesus there was a group of charlatans posing as faith healers and exorcists. These seven brothers apparently made their dishonest living by using the well-known religious vocabulary in order to perform exorcisms (v. 13). They used the names of Jesus and Paul, presumably to impress whoever was paying the bill for their services, but on this day the demons answered. In one swift and unexpected motion, the man with the evil spirit jumped on all seven brothers, overpowered them, and chased them out into the streets naked and bleeding (vv. 15–16). Luke apparently includes the story to highlight the demon's words, "I recognize Jesus, and I know about Paul" (v. 15).

The church of Jesus spread rapidly through the Roman Empire because Paul and others like him were so devoted to

Jesus. They became known in hell. With that kind of dedication and spiritual anointing upon their lives, no wonder the earliest missionaries "turned the world upside down" (Acts 17:6, ESV). With a similar devotion and the help of God's Spirit, our own world will see the continued spread of the message of Jesus today.

For Memory and Meditation

"For so the Lord has commanded us, 'I have placed You as a light for the Gentiles, that You may bring salvation to the end of the earth.'" Acts 13:47

Revelation—the Final Victory of Christ

Focal Text: Revelation 1–3

I once met a man who told me the book of Revelation is easy to understand. He was, however, in a minority. Most Bible students have, at some point, felt intimidated by the book's descriptions of previously unknown animals, obviously symbolic numbers, battles between angelic and demonic forces, and frightening warnings about the future. The book of Revelation is the most difficult book in the New Testament to interpret because the language is symbolic and the action unfolds like a tsunami of visions barely recognizable in our conscious or daily experience.

In spite of its difficulties, however, Revelation remains one of our favorite books and contains a specific promise of blessing for anyone who reads it (1:3). In addition, the reader is also warned about adding anything to the prophecy (22:18). With those two promises as a framework, we will attempt a brief overview of the seven churches that originally received this fascinating and inspired letter.

Regardless of the interpretive challenges, the book of Revelation has a clear purpose. To conclude that Revelation is about end times is only partially correct. More importantly, it is a book about our Lord's victory over all challenges and His sweeping plans through history to accomplish His will for Israel, the church, and the non-Christian world (11:15). Revelation is a fitting book to conclude the New Testament because it

91

declares emphatically that God's plan of redemption through Christ succeeds (21:1–7).

The Seven Churches
Revelation 1–3

The book is a "Revelation of Jesus Christ" given to show "the things which must soon take place" (1:1). While the book is the word of the Lord Jesus, it is conveyed through an angel and told to a Christian named John, regarded since antiquity as the apostle John, the disciple of Jesus and author of the Gospel of John and three small letters. He was imprisoned on "the island called Patmos because of the word of God and the testimony of Jesus," a fairly obvious description of having fallen victim to official religious persecution (1:9). The Romans used the small island (just six miles wide) as a penal colony for the empire's political prisoners.

The island of Patmos is forty-five miles from Ephesus in the Aegean Sea. Escape was impossible. The fact that John was a prisoner for being a Christian helps explain what the churches of the Roman Empire were experiencing. Christianity had once enjoyed official protection because Rome viewed it as a sect of Judaism, which they allowed. But sixty years had passed since the crucifixion of Jesus, and the political climate had cooled against the church. As a result persecution was common. This was part of the backdrop against which John wrote to seven churches, all clustered in a relatively small area of the biblical Asia Minor or what we know as modern-day Turkey. The entire region is familiar to the student of the New Testament because it follows a similar, though not exact, route as the mission trips of the apostle Paul. The region was among the first to be evangelized outside of Jewish circles and was the neighborhood of some of the first Gentile churches (Acts 14–19). In that way these seven churches represent a kind of headwater to all the churches that would follow for the next two thousand years. In them we catch a glimpse of our spiritual family tree.

On a particular Sunday, probably in the mid 90s AD, John was "in the Spirit" (Rev. 1:10), perhaps an indication of an attitude of worship and prayer, when he received a vision of the risen Lord Jesus (1:9–18). Jesus had a message for His church (1:11).

Ephesus (2:1–7)

The first message was to the church at Ephesus where the apostle Paul had planted a congregation decades earlier (Acts 19). In the first message to the church, we notice a pattern that stays mostly consistent in the six that follow. The Lord identifies Himself in a descriptive introduction, followed by commendation to the church for the good it has done, a rebuke for an intrinsic flaw, a call to repent, and a promise for those who heed the warnings. The exceptions to this pattern are found in the church in Smyrna (modern Ismir, Turkey), which received no rebuke (Rev. 2:8–11). Another exception to the general pattern is the church at Sardis, which received no commendation (Rev. 3:1–6). The church at Philadelphia likewise received no rebuke (Rev. 3:7–13), and the church at Laodicea received no commendation (Rev. 3:14–21), while the other elements of the pattern are present.

The messages to these churches had their origins in the historic circumstances particular to them, but for the last two millennia believers have easily found a message for their own times in each of the seven Turkish congregations. All of the churches, for instance, were enduring a period of struggle and challenge and some persecution. Every Christian and every congregation know how that feels, and these messages translate into our own times and circumstances as if they were written not to churches long ago and far away but to us now.

As Jesus introduces Himself to each congregation, He presents a different aspect of His character, which seems to relate directly to the issue addressed in that church. To the church in Ephesus, He was the One who "walks among the seven golden lampstands" (2:1). The "golden lampstands" had already been identified as the churches themselves (1:20). Therefore, Jesus is reminding Ephesus that He is near, actually in the midst of the church; yet Ephesus had "left" their "first love" (v. 4). The tragedy of a church or a Christian who has grown indifferent and unloving toward the Lord they once adored is that the Lord is still walking with them, yet ignored and unloved by them. The only remedy is repentance and a return to the fire of first love (v. 4).

Smyrna (2:8–11)

To the church at Smyrna, Jesus is described as "the first and the last, who was dead, and has come to life" (v. 8). This was an appropriate designation to remind and encourage a group of people suffering the threat of impending prison, persecution, and possible death sentences (v. 10). As the "first and the last," He reminded them that He has already seen the future (the last) and has conquered the death that threatens them. There is an arc to history, and it bends in the direction of victory for the believer even in the face of current suffering (vv. 10–11).

Pergamum (2:12–17)

Next Jesus addresses a church in horrible surroundings. Pergamum was a church where "Satan's throne is" (v. 13). What did

Jesus mean by "Satan's throne"? Satan is the spiritual enemy of Christ and His people, and he is eventually destroyed (Rev. 20:10). The word *Satan* means "adversary." Jesus had done battle with him and his army of demonic spirits throughout His ministry in Galilee and Jerusalem. To refer to Satan's throne is certainly to describe his headquarters or the seat of his kingdom. Was Pergamum more like hell than other cities? Or is Jesus speaking metaphorically to describe another adversary, one much easier to identify for the suffering church? Was Jesus referring to Rome? Was it the adversary Satan used to persecute the people of God?

Some active, evil force was attempting to force believers to renounce their faith and reject Christ (v. 13). Pergamum was a city filled with altars, temples, and the religious worship of Greek gods. But there was something else: Pergamum had an altar built to worship the Roman emperor. To this church that ministered "where Satan's throne is" (v.13), Jesus introduced Himself as the One with a "sharp two-edged sword" (v. 12). His church may dwell in a bad neighborhood, but the Lord is equipped and ready to protect the church no matter how intense the suffering.

Thyatira (2:18–29)

Thyatira was a city with an appetite for sexual immorality and false gods (v. 20). It was not unlike other cities in the Roman world (or postmodern America); they thrived on lucrative business deals (Acts 16:14) and physical pleasures (v. 21). The problem with the church in Thyatira was that it was willing to "tolerate" the spirit of immorality in their city (v. 20). The word *tolerate* means that they allowed it. Of course the church had no political power and little social influence so the idea of tolerance is that they did not preach against it. They turned a blind eye to the excesses of the city. However, the Lord does not, and He reminded the tolerant church that His "eyes are like a flame of fire" (v. 18), perhaps suggesting that His eyes never shut; they see everything that otherwise might be hidden or secret. Nothing is hidden from the "fire" of His scrutiny!

Sardis (3:1–6)

The church of Sardis needed a spiritual awakening: Jesus declared them dead (3:1). It was worse, in one sense, than a death sentence; they tried to convince themselves and the surrounding area that they were alive. They were spiritually inactive, ineffective, and in a spiritual coma (v. 2). Jesus did not deny their "deeds," which gave the church an appearance of health, presumably to the city as the works were regarded as a reputation (v. 1), but in terms of true spiritual health, all of their activity was meaningless and sinful (v. 3). Jesus reminds this lifeless church with its focus on external appearances that He will "come like a thief, and you will not know at what hour I will come" (v. 3). With that Jesus made clear to all of us that He is coming again. For a church or an individual believer on spiritual life support, a powerful, extrinsic motivating factor is this: someday Jesus will return to review our lives and ministry. Therefore, "wake up" (v. 2)!

In addition, the self-designation of Jesus to this congregation is one of life. He holds "the seven Spirits of God" (v. 1). The Spirit of God is life (Rom. 8:2, 10; 2 Cor. 3:6). What, though, is meant by the "seven Spirits of God" (v. 1)? No book of the New Testament relies more heavily on allusions and indirect references from the Old Testament than Revelation. The reference to "the seven Spirits" (also mentioned in John's introduction in

1:4; 5:6) is not simple to understand, but like other mysteries in the book of Revelation, we can look to the Old Testament for guidance.

The prophet Zechariah describes seeing a vision from "a lampstand all of gold" which had "seven lamps on it" (Zech. 4:2). When the prophet asked what it all meant, the Lord replied, "Not by might nor by power, but by My Spirit" (4:6). Apparently, the idea is that of the completeness of the Spirit of God. Isaiah likewise referred to "the Spirit of the Lᴏʀᴅ" which will rest upon the Messiah (Isa. 11:2). He then goes on to refer to "the Spirit" as the "Spirit of wisdom and understanding, . . . counsel and strength, . . . knowledge and the fear of the Lᴏʀᴅ" (11:2). Therefore, He has the title "the Spirit" and six other descriptions for a total of seven descriptive terms for the Holy Spirit (11:2–3). To the lifeless church at Sardis, Jesus reminded them He is the giver of spiritual life.

Philadelphia (3:7–13)

To the church of Philadelphia, Jesus has no rebuke. They were apparently a small congregation with limited physical resources (v. 8). These facts, however, have virtually nothing to do with the way the Lord sees them (v. 9). Jesus commends the fact that in spite of their physical limitations and obvious vulnerabilities, they heroically "kept" the word of the Lord and refused, presumably under duress, to deny the Lord (v. 8).

To this congregation, intimidated constantly by the political and social pressures closing in around them, Jesus reminded them that they were not boxed in after all; He holds the keys (v. 7). Their "little power" (v. 8), which seemed to be a limit and a closed door in their face, could be reversed in an instant by "an open door which no one can shut" (v. 8). Jesus promised them a "crown," a place in the "temple of My God" in "the new Jerusalem," and a "new name" (vv. 11–12). So for the faithful church with limits in the moment, the future could not look more promising!

Laodicea (3:14–22)

The last of the seven churches is the Laodicean congregation, which was full of problems. Jesus had nothing positive to say about this group. They were financially prosperous but spiritually bankrupt (v. 17). They were famously "lukewarm," a description that smacks of a distasteful condition so undesirable Jesus promised to spit them out like a man who unexpectedly tastes something terrible (vv. 15–16).

To this smug group of room-temperature Christians, Jesus presented Himself as "the Amen, the faithful and true Witness" (v. 14) and by inference shows Himself as the one truth their self-delusions could not deceive. What a church says about itself is not the final word on the subject. The Amen has the last word.

To these churches, and every church since, the Lord holds out hope and extends the promise of a victorious future that will come at the end (21:22–26). No matter what this present world does or says concerning the church, the book of Revelation is our constant reminder of ultimate victory.

For Memory and Meditation

"He who has an ear, let him hear what the Spirit says to the churches." Revelation 2:29

EPILOGUE

A proper understanding of the New Testament deserves and demands a lifetime of study and devotion. This brief survey gives the reader an overview of the most important document of the Christian life. Ultimately, time spent reading the New Testament is the best way to grasp its truth and have its truth grasp you. For instance, by reading only three chapters a day, you can easily complete the reading in less than ninety days. Every Christian who desires to grow as a disciple should read through the entire New Testament, along with more in-depth studies of the individual books. In this way you become more familiar with the Lord and His plan for humankind and His specific will for your life.

The New Testament applies to our lives today because it was not written in a vacuum, apart from real-life experiences. Instead, it was written at a time of rapid political and religious changes that affected the lives of its first readers. While the message of Scripture directly speaks to an audience in the twenty-first century, we can never accurately access the value of that message if it is removed from its original context. How can we understand the context of the New Testament? Several factors must be considered.

First, the apostles had seen the resurrected Christ, and as a result they had a miraculous story that insisted on being told. Apart from the historical fact of an empty tomb and the eyewitness accounts of Jesus' death and resurrection, there is no adequate explanation for the existence, let alone the rapid growth, of the early church. They were persecuted almost from the beginning, and only their certainty that He was alive again could have accounted for their faithfulness, even to the point of martyrdom.

That persecution, which was first expressed as religious oppression (Acts 8:1–2), soon became political or legal persecution as well. James, among the apostles, was executed first, and King Herod had hoped to execute Peter. Due to divine intervention Herod was unsuccessful (Acts 12:1–5). The legal hostility against the church continued throughout the period of the writing of the New Testament as is obvious from the descriptions of persecution evident against the churches even in Revelation, the last book written (Rev. 2:9–10). These events are always in the background (when they are not center stage) in the telling of the New Testament story.

A third concern that influenced the real situation in life of the New Testament letters was the prevalence of heresies. Almost immediately as churches were planted, heresy found a foothold in the thinking of some new believers (Gal. 1:6-9). Letters were written to encourage persecuted followers of Christ and to correct those who deviated from the teaching of Jesus and His apostles. Those real-world issues led to the writing of the books of the New Testament, and as a result, today Christians still find encouragement through our difficulties and correction when our thinking strays from the biblical message.

In order to help the reader feel at home in the first-century context, throughout this survey we have sought to include as much historical and geographical detail as can be ascertained from the text itself, so as to allow for meaningful application to life today. We are limited in this desire by the intentional nature of a survey. More study is warranted and will be available in anticipated future volumes of this series, which will cover individual books of the Bible in more detail.

In our quest to understand the New Testament, there are three additional factors to remember. First, while there are twenty-seven books, there are no more than nine authors.

Of those nine (Matthew, Mark, Luke, John, Paul, the author of Hebrews, James, Peter, and Jude), three are the most prominent, and their writings account for most of the New Testament. Paul, John and Luke wrote all but 71 of the 260 chapters in the New Testament. Therefore, almost 75 percent of the New Testament chapters were written by only three authors. A word count would make the percentages much more obvious as Luke, for instance, wrote the two longest books in the New Testament with unusually long chapters while Peter, James, and Jude wrote much shorter books and chapters and thus contributed fewer words. One chapter in the book of Luke could easily be the equivalent of several chapters in the books of James or 1 or 2 Peter. Since Luke was a protégé and traveling companion of Paul, it is natural to assume the influence of Paul's theology on Luke, thereby enhancing Paul's already obvious footprint on the life of the church for the last two thousand years.

The second factor of some importance in comprehending the New Testament is that the action takes place almost exclusively in three locations: Israel, modern-day Turkey, and part of modern-day Greece. The more one can understand about life for those people, in those places, and at that time, the better one can appreciate the message in its original context.

A third issue deals with the nature of the literature itself. The study of the New Testament cannot be separated from the fact that God chose to speak through the written word. Literary rules assist the interpreter. For instance, we cannot ignore the different literary genres represented. When the reader approaches the text, different rules apply for interpreting parables, for instance, than for interpreting epistles. In addition, the reader also finds narrative and apocalyptic literature in the New Testament, as well as direct and indirect quotations and allusions from the Old Testament. All of these literary types present unique interpretive challenges. Also, the New Testament was written in Greek, but the linguistic style and quality of the grammar and vocabulary differ from author to author. Keeping these things in mind can help the reader avoid pitfalls that have trapped others in doctrinal and factual errors in the past.

Almost forty years ago an evangelical phenomenon occurred in a subsection of the United States population. There was a revival among young people, and they were predominantly, although not exclusively, from the hippie counterculture. This national movement, which seemed to spring up spontaneously in areas as diverse as Southern California and Asbury, Kentucky, burst into full bloom in my own hometown of Fairbanks, Alaska. Hundreds of young people were swept into the kingdom in a matter of months. The young peoples' revival of the early 1970s has been called the Jesus Movement. I saw it. I was there.

Two thousand years earlier, the original Jesus Movement began, and it continues today. It was started by Jesus Himself, and His followers fanned it into a blaze that engulfed the Roman Empire in a single generation. The reality and importance of that movement were at the center of my thinking and at the core of my own personal perspective about the New Testament as I wrote this work. The next generation of the real Jesus Movement, started by Jesus along the shoreline of the Sea of Galilee, will be experienced first by those who study and teach the Bible. May God bless you as you study the New Testament and find yourself caught up in the continuing movement of Jesus.

For Teaching Helps
and Additional
Small Group Study
Materials Visit:
Auxanopress.com